FREQUENTLY ASKED CODING INTERVIEW

Part2: Algorithms

Rajini
Adhikesavan

To family, friends and teachers

PREFACE

Who are the intended audience?

This book provides frequently asked coding interview questions and answers for programmers preparing for job interviews. These questions and answers are intended for programmers and students with some java programming experience and are not for beginners who are just starting to learn programming. Java programmers can review and learn Algorithms and Data Structures along with other important concepts in preparation for a job interview.

Why this book?

There are many books and online tutorials available for coding interview preparation, but they are exhaustive in volume and content. This book provides concise and clear material on important topics that can be reviewed in a short period of time.

These coding questions and answers have been compiled from personal study materials collected over 15 years after interviewing with hundreds of silicon valley companies. After receiving positive feedback from friends and colleagues who successfully used this material to land a job, it has been compiled to the current format.

This is a sincere attempt to make coding interview preparation as simple and easy as possible.

What's in this book?

This book has simplified and distilled collection of frequently asked coding interview questions and answers.

Part 2 covers Java Algorithms and Data Structures. Part 1 covers Core Java Programming. There are 140+ questions in Algorithms and Data Structures. Core Java Programming package has 200+ questions.

How can I best use this book ?

Spending time on each question, answer, and answer explanation as well as going through the details thoroughly will ensure a complete understanding of the concepts covered.

Since many of the questions in specific categories are related, working on them together helps in a comprehensive coverage of related concepts.

Can I use this book to prepare for interviews with Google, Facebook, Apple, Microsoft or Amazon?

These coding interview questions and answers are designed for comprehensive coverage of important topics in java algorithms and data structures. This book is designed to be concise and clear providing one simple and efficient solution for a coding problem, although a problem can be solved using different methods.

Several topics and concepts have been broken down into smaller units with a clear solution and explanation. These solutions can be put together to solve similar or larger problems.

These coding interview questions and answers are designed for users to be able to review and master frequently asked questions in any software company.

Rajini Adhikesavan
San Francisco, CA
July, 2024

CONTENTS

ALGORITHMS &
DATA STRUCTURES

Data Structures and Algorithm Analysis

1.1 COMPLEXITY BASICS

1.1.1

Core application performance tuning can be performed by analyzing and working with

a. algorithms
b. data structures
c. data structures and algorithms
d. none of the above

Ans: c

Answer Explanation:

Memory usage and the CPU time for running a program depends on the data structures and algorithms used in a program.

Data structure is a way of organizing data. Algorithm is sequence of steps used to accomplish a task.

ArrayList, LinkedList and HashMap are examples of data structures. Linear search, binary search, LinkedList add and remove operations are all examples of algorithms.

1.1.2

What is algorithm complexity?

a. Amount of time and space required for increase in input.
b. Performance for increase in input
c. Scalability
d. All of the above

Ans: d

Answer Explanation:

Performance is the amount of time and space required for a given input.

Algorithmic complexity is about how an algorithm performs with increase in the input size. So, algorithmic complexity is about scalability.

Big-O notation or complexity usually refers to the worst-case scenario describing the time or space used.

1.1.3

What does Big-O notation represent?

a. performance
b. algorithm complexity
c. time complexity
d. space complexity

Ans: b

Answer Explanation:

Algorithmic complexity is also referred as asymptotic notation or Big-O notation.

If an algorithm should search through all the elements, it is called linear and it's Big-O is written as $O(n)$ where n is the number of elements.

Complexity can be constant, logarithmic, linear, quadratic, cubic or exponential.

1.1.4

Big-O or complexity usually describes

a. best-case scenario
b. worst-case scenario
c. average-case scenario

d. all of the above

Ans: b

Answer Explanation:

While looking at how the algorithm behaves with increase in data to process, the best-case, worst-case and average-case scenarios come into picture.

Among these, the worst-case scenario is of greater significance and sometimes the average case. The notation used to represent the worst-case findings is called Big-O represented by a capital "O".

If an algorithm should search through all the elements, it is called linear and its Big-O is written as $O(n)$, where n is the number of elements.
For linear search worst-case is n comparisons, best-case is 1 comparison and average-case is n/2 comparisons.

1.1.5

Algorithm complexity is about

a. time complexity
b. space complexity
c. time and space complexity
d. none of the above

Ans: c

Answer Explanation:

Time complexity is the time an algorithm takes to run for the data processed. Space complexity is the amount of memory used by the algorithm for the input data.

Time and space complexities determine the efficiency of an algorithm. Space complexity is ignored if the space used is minimal or if the space is constant irrespective of the items processed by the algorithm.

1.1.6

If an algorithm repeatedly subdivides the number of elements it has to search through, to find a value as in binary search, then it's said to be:

a. linear
b. logarithmic
c. quadratic
d. exponential

Ans: b

Answer Explanation:

Complexity for logarithmic runtime is O(log N). This examines the logarithm of the number of elements.

1.1.7

Following complexity does not depend on the size of input data:

a. linear
b. logarithmic
c. quadratic
d. constant

Ans: d

Answer Explanation:

Complexity for constant runtime is O(1). It takes constant steps for performing a given operation and execution time does not depend on the size of the input data. Example for constant complexity is adding an element to the front of a linked list.

1.1.8

Algorithms with following complexity perform very well with large size of input data:

a. linear
b. logarithmic
c. constant
d. all of the above

Ans: d

Answer Explanation:

Algorithms with constant, linear and logarithmic complexity perform well with input data size of about few hundred millions.

Quadratic works well for several thousand elements, while cubic for about thousand elements.

1.2 COMPLEXITY FOR PROGRAMS

1.2.1

1.
```
for(int i=0; i<n.length; i++) {

      System.out.println(n[i]);
}
```

2.
```
for(int i=0; i<n.length; i++) {

      for(int j=0; j<n.length; j++) {

            System.out.println(n[i] * n[j]);
      }
}
```

Complexity or Big-O notation for above two loops are:

a. O(1) and O(n)
b. O(log n) and O(n^2)
c. O(n) and O(n^2)
d. O(n) and O(log n)

Ans: c

Answer Explanation:

Algorithm analysis involves looking at how many times the elements are accessed in a loop or recursion.

In the first loop, the elements are accessed n times and runs linear or O(n) times.

In the second loop, the elements are accessed in the first and second loop for n^2 times and runs quadratic or O(n^2) times.

1.2.2

```
public static void printNumbers(int count) {

        int n = count;      //runs 1 time

        while(n>=1) {   //runs n+1 times including exit condition

                System.out.println(n);    //runs n times
                        n--;                          //runs n times

        }
}
```

Complexity for the above method is:

a. O(n)
b. O(n^2)
c. O(n^3)
d. O(log n)

Ans: a

Answer Explanation:

Time Complexity for the above code is:

$T(n) = a1 (1) + a2(n+1) + a3(n) + a4(n)$

$T(n) = (a1+a2) + n (a2+a3+a4)$

(a1+a2) and (a2+a3+a4) are constants and can be ignored

$T(n) = O(n)$

This is linear, as the elements are accessed n times.

Complexity is defined as a numerical function T(n) of time versus the input size n.

Since the same algorithm with the same input size may take different times to execute in different machines due to processor speed etc., we use asymptotic notation. a1, a2, a3 and a4 represent constants which may take different times in different machines.

Regardless of these constant values, T(n) grows linearly as the input size increases.

1.2.3

```
public static void printNumbers(int count) {

        int n = count;                    // runs 1 time
        while(n>=1) {
                // runs log n+2 times includes the following:
                // 1. number of times n is divided by 2 →  log n times
                // 2. when n=n → 1 time
                // 3. exit condition → 1 time
            System.out.println(n);    // log n+1
                    n = n/2;              // log n+1
        }
}
```

Complexity for the above loop is:

a. $O(n)$
b. $O(n^2)$
c. $O(n^3)$
d. $O(\log n)$

Ans: d

Answer Explanation:

Time Complexity for the above code is:

$T(n) = a1\ (1) + a2(\log n+2) + a3(\log n+1) + a4(\log n+1)$

$T(n) = (a1+2a2 +a3+a4) + \log n\ (a2+a3+a4)$

$(a1+2a2+a3+a4)$ and $(a2+a3+a4)$ are constants and can be ignored

$T(n) = O(\log n)$ which is logarithmic.

Reference for log base 2:

$2^k = n$
$\log(2^k) = \log n$
$k \log 2 = \log n$
$k = \log n$

Complexity is defined as a numerical function T(n) of time versus the input size n. Since the same algorithm with the same input size may take different times to execute in different machines due to processor speed etc. we use Big-O notation.

a1, a2, a3 and a4 represent constants which may take different times in different machines. Regardless of these constant values, T(n) grows logarithmically here, as the input size increases.

1.2.4

public static void printNumbers(int n) {

```
        int k = 1;                      // runs 1 time
        while(k <= n) {
                // runs log n+2 times includes the following:
                // 1. number of times k is multiplied by 2 →  log n times
                // 2. when k=n → 1 time
                // 3. exit condition → 1 time

                System.out.println(n);    // log n+1
                k = k * 2;                // log n+1
        }
}
```

Complexity for the above loop is:

a. O(n)
b. O(n^2)
c. O(n^3)
d. O(log n)

Ans: d

Answer Explanation:

Time Complexity for the above code is:

$T(n) = a1 (1) + a2(\log n+2) + a3(\log n+1) + a4(\log n+1)$

$T(n) = (a1+2a2 +a3+a4) + \log n (a2+a3+a4)$

(a1+2a2+a3+a4) and (a2+a3+a4) are constants and can be ignored.

$T(n) = O(\log n)$ which is logarithmic.

1.3 COMPLEXITY FOR ALGORITHMS

1.3.1

Complexity for Bubble Sort, Selection Sort and Insertion Sort is

a. O(n)
b. O(log n)
c. O(n log n)
d. O(n^2)

Ans: d

Answer Explanation:

Big-O for Bubble Sort, Selection Sort and Insertion Sort is O(n^2).

The advantage of using insertion sort over the other two sorting algorithms is that, insertion sort runs in linear time O(n) if the data is almost sorted.

1.3.2

Complexity for Heap Sort, Merge Sort and Quick Sort is

a. O(n)
b. O(log n)
c. O(n log n)
d. O(n^2)

Ans: c

Answer Explanation:

For quick sort, complexity for the worst-case is O(n^2), while complexity for average-case as well as best-case scenario is O(n log n).

For heap sort and merge sort best, average and worst case complexity is O(n log n).

Quick Sort:

Uses divide and conquer and uses partitioning for sorting data. Quick sort is an in place sort. Average case space complexity is O(log n).

Merge Sort:

Uses divide and conquer method. Data is divided, sorted and then merged. Using merge sort, different data sets can be sorted concurrently and then merged. It can be used for processing large amounts of data. Space complexity is O(n).

Merge sort can be used when data is huge but available memory is less. Data can be divided and then loaded into memory in chunks for sorting before they are merged.

Heap Sort:

Builds a heap out of the data set, removes the largest element and places in the end of a partially sorted array. Space complexity is O(1). Heap Sort moves data around a lot. Uses less extra memory for building a heap and can be used when memory available is less.

Among these three sorting algorithms, quick sort is fast when using arrays, merge sort works well for linked list and heap sort is the slowest. Merge sort is stable while quick sort and heap sort are not.

Although worst-case complexity for quick sort is O(n^2), it can be avoided by choosing the right pivot. Quick sort is faster than merge sort and heap sort. Since quick sort is an in place sort, it doesn't take up extra memory.

1.3.3

HashSet performs add() remove() and contains() methods in

a. Constant time or O(1)
b. Logarithmic time or O(log n)
c. Linear time or O(n)
d. Quadratic time or O(n^2)

Ans: a

Answer Explanation:

add() adds a new object to the Set, remove() removes a specified object from the Set and contains() returns a boolean value of true if the specified element is present in the Set or false otherwise.

HashSet performs the add, delete and search operations in constant time because of hashing. This is the best possible scenario as constant time algorithm always takes the same amount of time to run. Constant time would be the time to compute the hashcode and operate on the element.

1.3.4

The TreeSet performs add() remove() and contains() methods in

a. Constant time or O(1)
b. Logarithmic time or O(log n)
c. Linear time or O(n)
d. Quadratic time or O(n^2)

Ans: b

Answer Explanation:

In a binary tree, the search algorithm repeatedly subdivides the number of elements it has to search through to find a value. TreeSet in java is a binary tree and time for add, remove and search takes O(log n)

1.3.5

Search and delete in array or ArrayList takes

a. Constant time or O(1)
b. Logarithmic time or O(log n)
c. Linear time or O(n)
d. Quadratic time or O(n^2)

Ans: c

Answer Explanation:

Insert and delete in Array or ArrayList takes linear time as all the elements may have to be traversed in the worst-case scenario of the element being the last.

1.3.6

Insert in an array or ArrayList takes

a. Constant time or O(1)
b. Logarithmic time or O(log n)
c. Linear time or O(n)
d. Quadratic time or O(n^2)

Ans: a

Answer Explanation:

Usually an element is inserted at the end of an array, so it takes constant time or O(1). In some scenarios when an element has to be inserted at the beginning of an array, then it takes linear time or O(n) as all the elements may have to be accessed to rearrange the positions.

ArrayList is a dynamic array where the array size is resized when the size is exceeded during inserts. This resizing is an expensive operation, but helps to gain constant time inserts.

1.3.7

Locating an element in a LinkedList takes

a. Constant time or O(1)
b. Logarithmic time or O(log n)
c. Linear time or O(n)
d. Quadratic time or O(n^2)

Ans: c

Answer Explanation:

Because of the underlying data structure, for locating an element in a LinkedList all elements may have to be examined which is linear time or $O(n)$. For insert and delete operations it takes constant time $O(1)$, as insert and delete operations are performed at the end of the list.

LinkedList uses the exact amount of memory to store data. When new elements are added, a new Entry is created and positioned appropriately in the LinkedList.

1.3.8

Best-case and worst-case performance of HashMap insert, delete and search is

a. $O(1)$ and $O(\log n)$
b. $O(1)$ and $O(n)$
c. $O(\log n)$ and $O(n)$
d. $O(n)$ and $O(n^2)$

Ans: b

Answer Explanation:

Since hash table is an array of linked list. The best case scenario is when there is no hash collision and the performance is $O(1)$.

The Map data structure stores key/value pairs. The hash or comparison function is applied only to the key and not the value. When an entry is accessed using the hash code, it's same as accessing an array with the index and the time to access is constant or $O(1)$.

The worst-case scenario is when there is hash collision and all the elements are in the same bucket and the performance is same as a linked list with complexity as $O(n)$.

1.4 CHOOSING DATA STRUCTURES

1.4.1

If an application requires adding all the elements, followed by random access using indexes, which of the following data structure will be the most suitable?

a. ArrayList
b. LinkedList
c. HashSet
d. HashMap

Ans: a

Answer Explanation:

ArrayList maintains the order for the elements by index position.

ArrayList stores memory in contiguous memory location. If an element is removed from the middle of the ArrayList, all the other elements have to be moved up. Same issue is with inserting an element also. This makes adding and removing elements in the middle of an ArrayList expensive.

Accessing an element by using array index is a very fast operation. If there is not much of add and delete operations, but more of access operations using the index position, then ArrayList can be used.

```
List<String> arrayList = new ArrayList<String>();
arrayList.add("a");
arrayList.add("b");
arrayList.add("c");

System.out.println("arrayList: " + arrayList);
System.out.println("arrayList.get(0): " + arrayList.get(0));
System.out.println("arrayList.get(1): " + arrayList.get(1));
```

Output:

arrayList: [a, b, c]

arrayList.get(0): a
arrayList.get(1): b

1.4.2

Difference between Array and ArrayList

1. Arrays have fixed size while ArrayList have dynamic size, keeps growing if needed.
2. Array can contain Objects and primitive types while ArrayList can have only Objects as elements.
3. While creating an instance of ArrayList, it's not necessary to specify the size but for Array, the size needs to be specified.
4. For adding or getting elements, ArrayList is slightly faster than Arrays.
5. ArrayList resize operation may slow down performance.

a. All of the above statements are true
b. All except 4 are true
c. All except 5 are true
d. All except 4 and 5 are true

Ans: b

Answer Explanation:

Following is an array declaration:

int [] array = new int[10];
array[10] = 2;

If the array index accessed exceeds the capacity as shown above, ArrayIndexOutOfBoundsException is thrown. While declaring an array, the size of the array should be specified. Array has fixed length, once the size is specified, it cannot be changed.

array[10] = 2;

ArrayIndexOutOfBoundsException is thrown. Since the size of the array is 10, the indexes from 0 to 9 are valid and 10 is not a valid index.

List<Integer> arrayList = new ArrayList<Integer>();

As shown in the ArrayList declaration above, size of the ArrayList is optional.

List<Integer> arrayList2 = new ArrayList<Integer>(1);
arrayList2.add(10);
arrayList2.add(20);
arrayList2.add(30);
System.*out*.println("arrayList2: " + arrayList2);

Output:

arrayList2: [10, 20, 30]

Size of the ArrayList is optional and need not be specified. When the size is specified as 1 and is exceeded as shown above, the size of the ArrayList is increased internally.

ArrayList has dynamic allocation of more memory when more elements are being added and the size of the existing allocated memory is not enough.

Array resize operation may slow down performance as a new ArrayList with a larger capacity is created and all the elements from the existing ArrayList is copied to the new one.

Array can take primitive types like int or objects, while ArrayList takes only objects like String, Integer etc.

Array is used if the number of elements are fixed and will not change. If array size may change and the number of input elements cannot be pre determined, then ArrayList can be used.

1.4.3

If frequent insert and delete operations are required at end of the list and not much of access to elements, the following data structure can be used:

a. ArrayList
b. LinkedList
c. HashSet
d. HashMap

Ans: b

Answer Explanation:

LinkedList linkedList = **new** LinkedList();
linkedList.add("a");
linkedList.add("b");
linkedList.add("c");
linkedList.remove("a");
System.*out*.println("linkedList: " + linkedList);

Output:

linkedList: bc

LinkedList implement the List interface in which elements are ordered.

LinkedList stores the elements in a separate link and each link has a reference to the next link. This way, insertion and deletion in the middle of the link is not expensive.

When an element is removed, simply the reference of the previous link is changed.

Searching in a linked list is a slow operation as all the elements have to be traversed. So, traversing to an element to be added or deleted is still a slow operation.

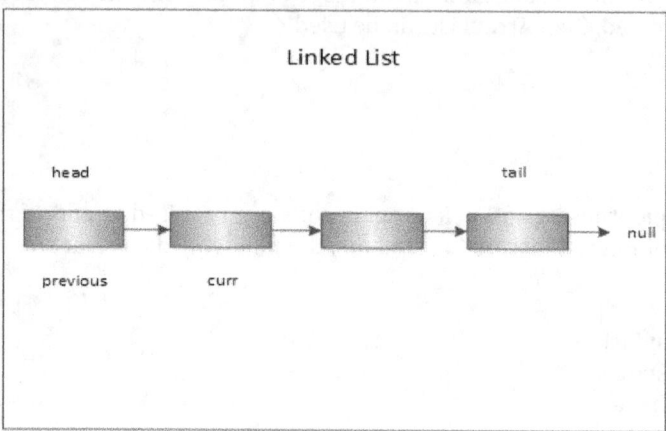

LinkedLists can be used for implementing stacks and queues since elements can be added or deleted quickly at the end of the linked list.

LinkedLists are rarely used, as ArrayLists (dynamic arrays) offer speed and flexibility compared to LinkedLists.

1.4.4

The following data structure is used for implementing a Last in First Out (LIFO) functionality

a. ArrayList
b. LinkedList
c. Stack
d. Queue

Ans: c

Answer Explanation:

Stack supports three operations

1. adding an element to the top of the stack called 'push'.
2. removing an element from the top of the stack called 'pop'.
3. examining the element at the top called 'peek'.

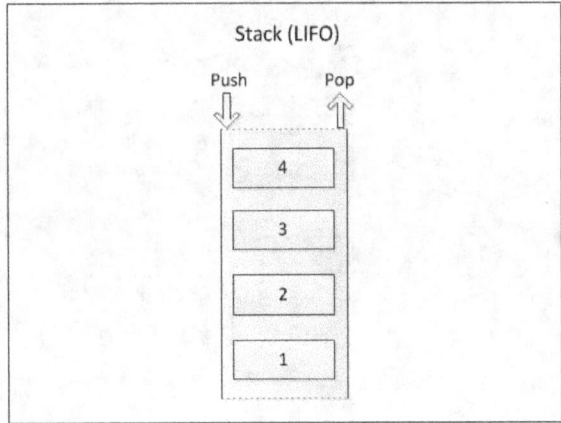

The push, pop and peek operations are very fast and require constant time.

1.4.5

The following data structure is used for implementing a First in First Out (FIFO) functionality

a. HashSet
b. TreeSet
c. Stack
d. Queue

Ans: d

Answer Explanation:

Queue supports two operations

1. adding an element to the tail called 'enqueue'.
2. removing an element from the head called 'dequeue'.

Both enqueue and dequeue operations are very fast and require constant time.

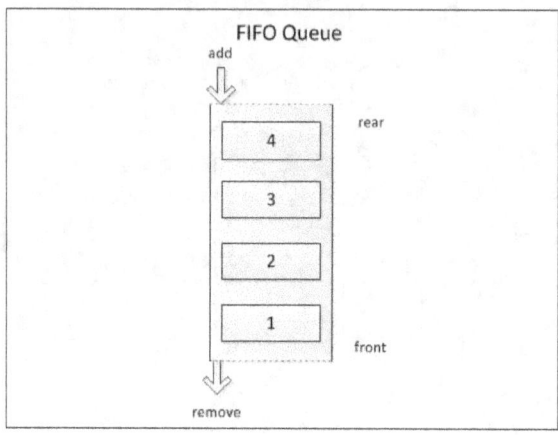

LinkedList is used to implement a Queue. Since Queue implements a FIFO functionality, it can be used for processing tasks in the order they were added to the Queue.

1.4.6

HashTable is a

a. Array
b. LinkedList
c. Array of LinkedList
d. ArrayList

Ans: c

Answer Explanation:

The hash table is an array of linked lists. Each list is called a bucket.

Hash table is a data structure for finding objects quickly. The hash table computes an integer called hashcode for each object, using the hashCode() function provided by either the object (eg: String object) or its base class, Object.

Once hash code is computed, hash code modulo the total number of buckets gives the index of the bucket where the element should be stored. If the hash code of the object is 449 and the total number of buckets is 121, the reminder of 449 divided by 121 gives 71. So the object is placed in bucket 71.

If there is no other element in this bucket, then the object is inserted. But if there are elements already in this bucket, it's called hash collision. The new object has to be compared with all the objects in the bucket to check if there is a match to avoid duplicate key entries.

If the hash codes are randomly distributed and if the number of buckets are large enough, then few hash comparisons will be needed.

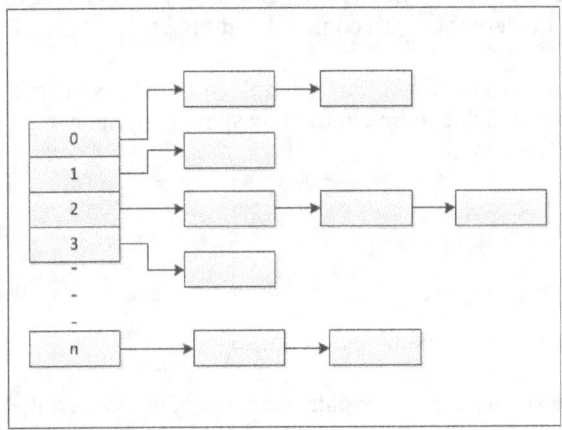

HashTable stores key, value pairs and has very fast add, remove and search of elements with constant complexity.

If there is a hash collision, then complexity for these three operations will be linear which can be avoided with correct bucket size during initialization.

HashTable can be used when quick search and addition functionalities are required. HashTable represents a dictionary data structure.

1.4.7

If the application requires to use an unordered collection without duplicates that doesn't require access by index, which of the following can be used

a. ArrayList
b. LinkedList
c. HashSet
d. HashMap

Ans: c

Answer Explanation:

Set is an unordered collection with no duplicates. All elements in a Set are unique. Set internally uses HashTable to store only the values that are hashed. Similar to HashTable, HashSet has very fast add, remove and search of elements with constant complexity.

If there is a hash collision, then complexity for these three operations will be linear which can be avoided by specifying the correct size when initializing the HashSet.

1.4.8

Difference between HashMap and HashSet

1. HashMap stores key/value pair while HashSet stores only the value.
2. Duplicate values are allowed for HashMap but not for HashSet.
3. For HashMap, hash code value is calculated using key object, while for HashSet, hash code value is calculated using value object.
4. Both allow null values and are not synchronized.

Which of the above statements are true?

a. All except 3
b. All except 4
c. All except 3 and 4

d. All of the above

Ans: d

Answer Explanation:

```
Set<String> hSet = new HashSet<String>();
hSet.add("a");
hSet.add("b");
hSet.add("c");
hSet.add("a");
hSet.add(null);

System.out.println("hSet: " + hSet);

Map<Integer, String> hMap = new HashMap<Integer, String>();
hMap.put(1, "a");
hMap.put(2, "b");
hMap.put(3, "c");
hMap.put(4, "a");
hMap.put(null, null);

System.out.println("hMap: " + hMap);
```

Output:

```
hSet: [null, b, c, a]
hMap: {null=null, 1=a, 2=b, 3=c, 4=a}
```

In the above sample, HashSet takes only values and HashMap takes key/value pairs. Also, both HashSet and HashMap take null values.

When duplicate value "a" is added to hSet, it is not stored. When duplicate value "a" is put in hMap with key 4, it is stored as shown in the output.

HashSet implements the Set interface and HashMap the Map interface. Both Set and Map are unordered collections. Set stores only values while Map stores key/value pairs.

Set does not allow duplicate values while Map allows duplicate values. For HashSet, hash code is computed using the value object and for HashMap using key object.

1.4.9

If the key value specified in get() method of HashMap is not found, the following value is returned

a. null
b. empty string
c. random value
d. none of the above

Ans: a

Answer Explanation:

If the key passed to the get() method of HashMap is not found, then null is returned.

```
Map<Integer, String> hMap = new HashMap<Integer, String>();
hMap.put(1, "a");
hMap.put(2, "b");
hMap.put(3, "c");
hMap.put(4, "d");

System.out.println("hMap.get(5): " + hMap.get(5));
```

Output:

hMap.get(5): null

1.4.10

```
Map<String, Aircraft> hMap = new HashMap<String, Aircraft>();

hMap.put("34892", new Aircraft("Boeing 727));
```

If the key 34892 is already present in hMap with an existing value:

a. the existing value remains unchanged
b. new value in the put method replaces the existing value

c. put method is not executed
d. none of the above
Ans: b

Answer Explanation:

Map<Integer, String> hMap = **new** HashMap<Integer, String>();
hMap.put(1, "a");
hMap.put(2, "b");
hMap.put(3, "c");
hMap.put(4, "d");
System.*out*.println("hMap: " + hMap);

hMap.put(1, "z");
System.*out*.println("hMap: " + hMap);

Output:

hMap: {1=a, 2=b, 3=c, 4=d}
hMap: {1=z, 2=b, 3=c, 4=d}

In the above sample, when key value pair of 1 and, z are added to hMap using put() method, z replaces the existing value a.

1.4.11

Following data structure can be used for storing key value pairs with key in sorted order

a. HashMap
b. TreeMap
c. HashSet
d. TreeSet

Ans: b

Answer Explanation:

Elements of a TreeMap are stored in a Tree. TreeMap represents a sorted dictionary data structure.

TreeMap provides fast execution of add, delete and search operation with logarithmic complexity.

If there are 1000 elements log2(1000) will be 10. For a TreeMap with 1000 elements, it would take 10 steps to perform add, delete or search operations.

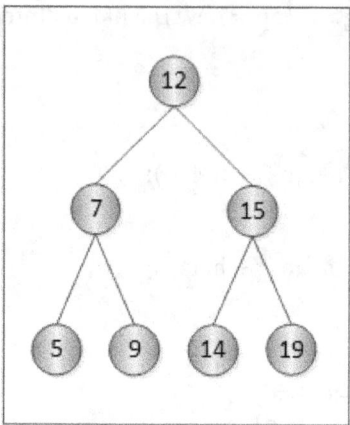

TreeMap which is a sorted dictionary data structure can be used for storing sorted key values which require fast search and add operations.

1.4.12

Search in a TreeSet takes

a. Constant time or O(1)
b. Linear time or O(n)
c. Quadratic time or O(n^2)
d. Logarithmic time or O(log n)

Ans: d

Answer Explanation:

TreeSet is a sorted collection with no duplicates. TreeSet internally uses a Tree data structure.

The complexity for add, delete and search operation for TreeSet which is a sorted set is logarithmic.

TreeSet can be used when unique elements need to be sorted and saved and can be accessed and added quickly.

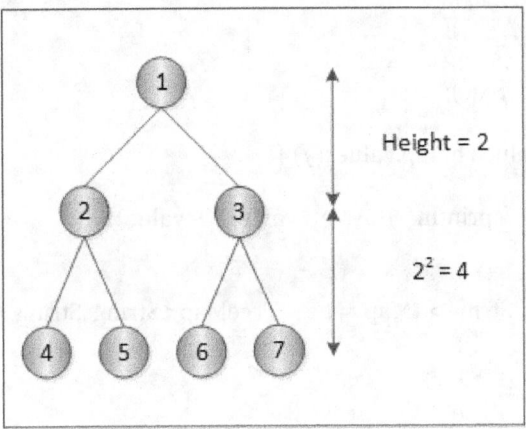

1.4.13

Difference between HashMap and TreeMap

1. HashMap elements are stored in a hash table while TreeMap elements are stored in a tree.
2. HashMap is unsorted, there is no ordering of key or values, while TreeMap is sorted and the elements are ordered by keys.
3. Adding an element to HashMap is faster than adding to TreeMap.
4. Keys added to HashMap should have hashCode() implementation while the keys added to TreeMap should be sortable, which can be specified in a comparator interface.

Which of the above statements are true?

a. All except 3
b. All except 4
c. All of the above
d. None of the above

Ans: c

Answer Explanation:

```
Map<String, String> hMap = new HashMap<String, String>();
hMap.put("a", "a");
hMap.put("b", "b");
hMap.put("c", "c");
hMap.put("d", "d");

for(String value : hMap.values()) {

    System.out.println("HasMap value: " + value);
}

Map<String, String> tMap = new TreeMap<String, String>();
tMap.put("c", "c");
tMap.put("b", "b");
tMap.put("d", "d");
tMap.put("a", "a");

for(String value : tMap.values()) {

    System.out.println("TreeMap value: " + value);
}
```

Output:

HasMap value: d
HasMap value: b
HasMap value: c
HasMap value: a

TreeMap value: a
TreeMap value: b
TreeMap value: c
TreeMap value: d

Both HashMap and TreeMap implement the Map interface and are not synchronized. Both don't allow duplicate keys. HashMap allows null values for key and value while TreeMap allows null for value only.

HashMap is implemented as a hash table. HashMap is an unordered collection used when ordering of the elements doesn't matter and provides fast lookup.
The elements in a TreeMap are stored in a tree and the elements can be retrieved in a sorted order as specified using the Comparable or Comparator interface. TreeMap is slower than HashMap.

1.4.14

Difference between ConcurrentHashMap, synchronizedMap and Hash table

1. ConcurrentHashMap is faster than Hashtable or synchronizedMap.
2. ConcurrentHashMap locks only portion of the Map instead of the whole Map like Hashtable or synchronizedMap
3. ConcurrentHashMap is best suited for a multi-threaded environment with multiple readers and few writers.
4. ConcurrentHashMap allows null as key or value.

Which of the above statements are true?

a. All except 3
b. All except 4
c. All except 3 and 4
d. All of the above

Ans: b

Answer Explanation:

Hashtable is a synchronized collection class and is obsolete. Collections.synchronizedMap() returns an instance of a synchronized wrapper class.

Map synchMap = Collections.*synchronizedMap*(hashMap);

The static synchronizedMap() method of the Collections class turns hashMap into a synchronized Map, synchMap with all the accessor methods synchronized. The synchronized get() and put() methods acquire a lock on synchMap.

synchMap is an object of a class that implements the Map interface and whose methods manipulate the methods of the original Map. This is called a view or a wrapper.
While iterating through synchMap, it needs to be synchronized, this is because only the accessor methods of the Map interface are synchronized but the original Collection object is not.

Also in a multi threaded environment, while iterating through any map, an object level lock should be acquired, otherwise if any other thread tries to modify the map at the same time, ConcurrentModification Exception is thrown.

```
synchronized(synchMap) {

    Iterator iter = synchMap.iterator();

    while(iter.hasNext()) {
        ...
    }
}
```

Locking this entire collection is a performance overhead, when one method acquires a lock on synchMap, other methods cannot access it.
ConcurrentHashMap solves this problem by providing fine grain locking and not holding a lock on the entire Map, so concurrent reads and writes are possible.

ConcurrentHashMap does not throw ConcurrentModificationException when a thread is iterating over it and another thread modifies the hashMap at the same time. This is because the iterator returned by ConcurrentHashMap is a snapshot of the data.

ConcurrentHashMap is designed for highly concurrent applications. ConcurrentHashMap allows different threads to access different parts of the Map simultaneously.

The Map is split internally into multiple parts depending on the concurrency level specified in the constructor. The default value of 16 for concurrency level will allow 16 concurrent updates on the hashMap.

As indicated above, ConcurrentHashMap has a lot of overhead in terms of memory and processor and should be used only in highly concurrent applications. For others, synchronized HashMap is a better choice.

1.4.15

To preserve the order of the elements in the sequence they are inserted, the following Collection can be used:

a. Set
b. SortedSet
c. LinkedHashSet
d. TreeSet

Ans: c

Answer Explanation:

LinkedHashSet maintains the insertion order.

```
Set<String> hSet = new HashSet<String>();
hSet.add("a");
hSet.add("b");
hSet.add("c");
hSet.add("d");
hSet.add(null);
System.out.println("hSet: " + hSet);

Set<String> lhSet = new LinkedHashSet<String>();
lhSet.add("a");
lhSet.add("b");
lhSet.add("c");
lhSet.add("d");
lhSet.add(null);
System.out.println("lhSet: " + lhSet);
```

Output:

hSet: [null, d, b, c, a]
lhSet: [a, b, c, d, null]

Both HashSet and LinkedHashSet implement the Set interface and don't allow duplicates. They allow null values as shown above and both use equals() method for comparison.

HashSet internally uses HashMap and LinkedHashSet internally uses LinkedHashMap.
HashSet is faster than LinkedHashSet as LinkedHashSet has to maintain a doubly linked list for insert and delete.

1.4.16

In a balanced binary tree, the largest element will be

a. last left node of the left branch of the tree.
b. last right node of the right branch of the tree.
c. last left node of the right branch of the tree.
d. last right node of the left branch of the tree.

Ans: b

Answer Explanation:

In a balanced binary tree, the largest element will be at the last right node of the right branch of the tree. The next largest node will be the left leaf of this branch. If the left leaf is not present, then it would be it's parent node.

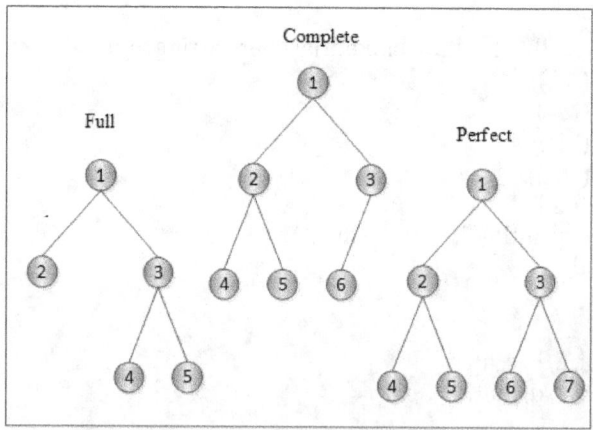

Binary Tree is a tree where every node has zero, one or two children.

Full Binary Tree:
Every node other than the leaves have two children. Leaves are nodes without any children.

Complete Binary Tree:
A binary tree in which every level is completely filled except possibly the last and all nodes are as far left as possible.

Perfect Binary Tree:
A full binary tree in which all nodes have two children and leaves are at the same depth.

In a binary search tree, all left subtree elements should be less than the root data and all right subtree elements should be greater than the root data. In a balanced tree, depth of the left and right subtrees of every node differ by 1 or less.

1.4.17

A heap stores data in a complete binary tree such that all children are

a. less than the parent
b. greater than the parent
c. less or greater than the parent
d. none of the above

Ans: c

Answer Explanation:

A heap stores data in a complete binary tree and all children of a parent are either less than or greater than the parent. The numbers are all either decreasing or increasing as you go down the tree.

Heap is an implementation of Priority Queue. Priority Queue supports insert and delete of min or max element in a data structure.

Min Heap:
The value of a node must be less than or equal to the values of its children. Used for sorting elements in ascending order.

Max Heap:
The value of a node must be greater than or equal to the values of its children. Used for sorting elements in descending order.

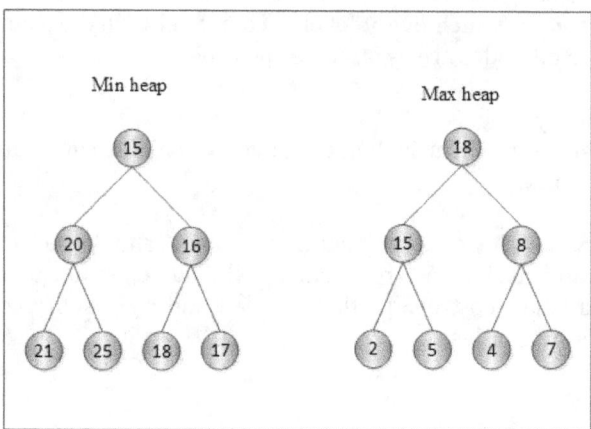

1.4.18

A min Heap stores data in a complete binary tree and the root node has the

a. minimum value
b. maximum value
c. minimum or maximum value
d. none of the above

Ans: a

Answer Explanation:

A min heap stores data in a complete binary tree and the value of a node must be less than or equal to the values of its children. Min heap is used for sorting elements in ascending order.

For min heap, root node has the minimum value in the tree. Min heap is an implementation of Priority Queue. Priority Queue supports insert and delete of min or max element in a data structure.

1.4.19

Which of the following data structure will be most efficient for storing and searching all words in a dictionary

a. HashMap
b. Binary Search Tree
c. Graph
d. Tries

Ans: d

Answer Explanation:

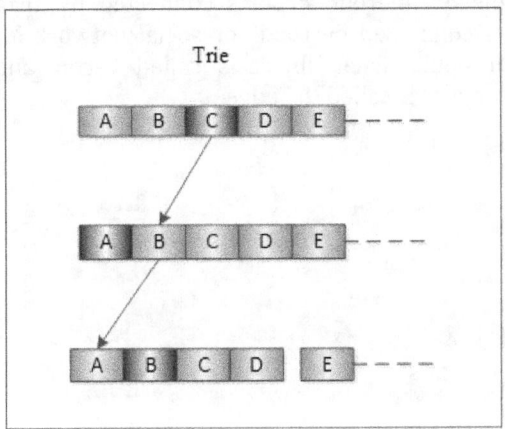

Tries are data structures based on prefix of a string. They are used for Re'trie'val of data. It's a multiway tree where each node can contain up to 26 children, 26 letters of the English alphabet.

Complexity for insert and search string in a Trie is O(L), where L is the length of the word. Insert and search operation in Tries are very fast but it requires a lot of memory as each node has too many children.

HashMap and Binary Search Tree can store each string, but string comparison at every node makes it slow for a large set of dictionary words.

1.4.20

A sparse graph has relatively few

a. vertices
b. edges
c. paths
d. cycles

Ans: b

Answer Explanation:

Graphs are used for representing objects and connections between them. Example is different airports connected by an airline route, different cities connected by roads or social network for people like twitter or facebook. Each object is called vertex and connection between two objects is called the edge.

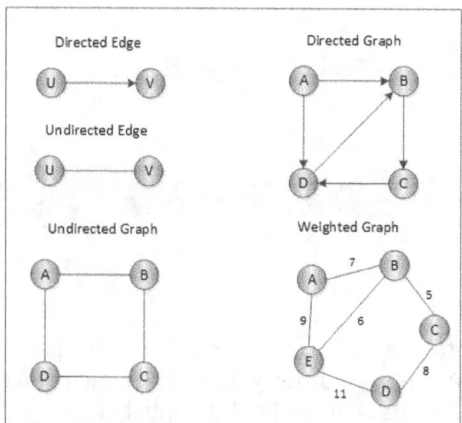

Directed edge:
First vertex u is the origin and the second vertex v is the destination. Ordered pair of vertices are represented as (u,v) which represents an edge.

Undirected edge:

Unordered pair of vertices represented as (u,v)

Directed graph:
Has all edges directed where the origin and destination vertices are indicated by an arrow.

Undirected graph:
Has all edges undirected. Unordered pair of vertices are represented as (u,v) which represents an edge.

In weighted graphs, integers are assigned to each edge to represent distances or costs.

Path is a sequence of adjacent vertices and a cycle is a path where first and last vertices are the same.

Graphs are usually represented using

1. Adjacency Matrix
2. Adjacency List

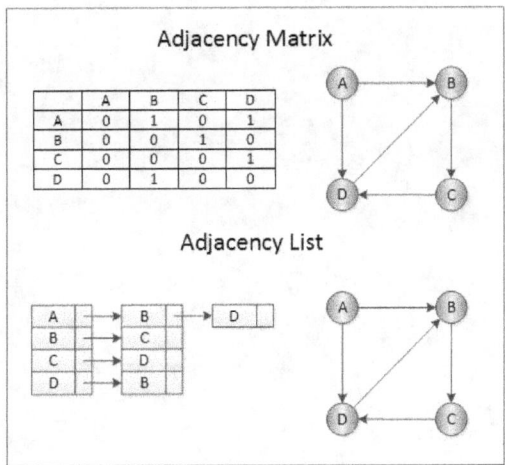

Adjacency Matrix:
Adjacency Matrix uses a matrix with size V x V which is represented by a two dimensional array adj[i][j].

when adj[i][j] is set to 1 if there is an edge from vertex i to vertex j, otherwise it's set to 0.

For a weighted graph, adj[i][j] is set to w, where w is the weight for the edge from vertex i to vertex j.

Adjacency List:
Adjacency List is represented by a array of linked list. Size of the array represents the number of vertices. So each vertex has a linked list and each list node represents the edge between this vertex and other vertices.

1.5 COLLECTION FUNCTIONALITIES

1.5.1

Aircraft [] aircraftArr = new Aircraft[20];

List<Aircraft> aircraftList = Arrays.*asList*(aircraftArr);

In the above code snippet,

1. aircraftList is not an ArrayList.
2. aircraftList is a view object with accessor methods accessing the underlying array.
3. Any aircraftList method that changes the size of the array like add and remove throws UnsupportedOperationException

Which of the above statements are true?

a. 2 and 3
b. 1 and 3
c. 1 and 2
d. 1, 2, and 3

Ans: d

Answer Explanation:

aircraftList object returned is not an instance of java.util.ArrayList but is an instance of java.util.Arrays$ArrayList class. This is ArrayList class which is a private static inner class of Arrays class.

aircraftList is a wrapper which wraps the get() and set() methods of the original Array.

When add() and remove() methods are called, Unsupported Operation Exception is thrown.

1.5.2

List dList = aList.subList(5, 10);

dList.clear();

In the above code snippet, dList.clear() method,

a. clears all elements of dList but doesn't affect aList.
b. clears all elements of dList and clears the subList specified for aList.
c. Does not clear dList or subList of aList.
d. None of the above.

Ans: b

Answer Explanation:

```
List<String> aList = new ArrayList<String>();
aList.add("a");
aList.add("b");
aList.add("c");
aList.add("d");

List dList = aList.subList(1, 3);
System.out.println("aList: " + aList + " dList: " + dList);
dList.clear();
System.out.println("After clearing, aList: " + aList + " dList: " + dList);
```

Output:

aList: [a, b, c, d] dList: [b, c]
After clearing, aList: [a, d] dList: []

In the above sample,

subList(int fromIndex, int toIndex)

is the signature of the subList() method that returns a sub list of the original list with fromIndex inclusive and toIndex exclusive.

From the original list aList, a subList dList is created for indices 1 and 2 with values b and c. Then a call to dList.clear() clears the subList in both the dList and the original List aList.

dList is a view of the original List aList and hence the clear operation happens on both the lists. To clear sublist of the original list directly, the following statement can be used.

```
aList.subList(1, 3).clear();
```

1.5.3

```
Map<String, Aircraft> aircraftMap =
    new HashMap<String, Aircraft>();

Set<String> aircraftIdSet = new HashSet<String>();
....
....
aircraftMap.keySet().removeAll(aircraftIdSet);
```

The above snippet removes the aircraftIdSet elements from

a. aircraftMap
b. keyset
c. both
d. none of the above

Ans: a

Answer Explanation:

Since the keySet is a view to the map, the keys (aircraftId) and associated aircraft objects are removed from the map.

```
Map<Integer, String> hMap = new HashMap<Integer, String>();
hMap.put(1, "a");
hMap.put(2, "b");
hMap.put(3, "c");
hMap.put(4, "d");
System.out.println("hMap: " + hMap);

Set<Integer> hSet = new HashSet<Integer>();
hSet.add(2);
hSet.add(3);
System.out.println("hSet: " + hSet);

hMap.keySet().removeAll(hSet);
System.out.println("After remove....");
System.out.println("hMap: " + hMap);
```

Output:

hMap: {1=a, 2=b, 3=c, 4=d}
hSet: [2, 3]
After remove....
hMap: {1=a, 4=d}

1.5.4

Set xSet = ...;
Set ySet = ...;

Set aSet = **new** HashSet(xSet);
aSet.retainAll(ySet);

After executing the above code, aSet will have

a. Contents of xSet
b. Contents of ySet
c. Contents of both xSet and ySet
d. Intersection of contents in xSet and ySet

Ans: d

Answer Explanation:

Set<String> xSet = **new** HashSet<String>();
xSet.add("a");
xSet.add("b");
xSet.add("c");

Set<String> ySet = **new** HashSet<String>();
ySet.add("b");
ySet.add("c");
ySet.add("d");

Set zSet = **new** HashSet(xSet);
zSet.retainAll(ySet);

System.*out*.println("xSet: " + xSet);
System.*out*.println("ySet: " + ySet);

System.*out*.println("zSet: " + zSet);

Output:

xSet: [b, c, a]
ySet: [d, b, c]
zSet: [b, c]

In the above code zSet is initialized with contents of xSet. Call to zSet.retainAll(ySet) saves all the values that are intersection of xSet and ySet into zSet as shown in the result.

1.5.5

Which of the following functions are supported by Collections class?

static Object min(Collection elements)
static Object max(Collection elements)
static Object min(Collection elements, Comparator c)
static Object max(Collection elements, Comparator c)
static void copy(List to, List from)
static void fill(List l, Object value)
static void reverse(List l)

a. All of the above
b. None of the above
c. min and max only
d. copy, fill and reverse only

Ans: a

Answer Explanation:

max and min elements are returned according to the ordering of the elements, so all elements should implement the Comparable interface.

For elements defined that do not implement the Comparable interface, max or min methods that use Comparator object as second parameter can be used.

In the copy() method, contents of "from" list is copied to the "to" list. In the fill() method, contents of List l is replaced by the element "value". Ordering of the elements in the list are reversed using the reverse() method .

1.5.6

Following are the functions supported by Collections class

static void sort(List list)
static void sort(List list, Comparator c)

List aList = ----;
Collections.sort(aList, Collections.reverseOrder());

Running the above code,

a. gives compiler error
b. throws exception
c. sorts aList in reverseOrder
d. sorts aList

Ans: c

Answer Explanation:

The static method sort() of the Collections class with one List parameter should have the object in the List implement Comparable interface.

Collections.sort(List l)

The sort method can also take a second parameter if the object doesn't implement the Comparable interface.   The second parameter Comparator is used to define the ordering of the elements.

Collections.sort(List l, Comparator c)

Collections.reverseOrder() returns a Comparator that imposes the reverse ordering of the specified comparator. In the method call below, aList will get sorted in reverse order provided the objects used in aList implement the Comparable interface.

Collections.sort(aList, Collections.reverseOrder());

1.5.7

List aList = ---;
Collections.shuffle(Collections.*unmodifiableList*(aList));

The above code snippet

a. Won't compile
b. Throws UnSupportedOperationException
c. Shuffles aList elements randomly
d. Does not shuffle aList elements

Ans: b

Answer Explanation:

The shuffle() method of the Collections class shuffles the elements of a list. Since the unmodifiable list cannot be shuffled, UnSupportedOperationException will be thrown.

1.6 DATA STRUCTURES FOR FUNCTIONS

1.6.1

An input file contains a list of student name followed by the course taken.

Jim | Physics
Alex | Math
Newton | Chemistry
Bruce | Art
Kelly |Physics
George | Math
Bruce | Physics

Each student can take multiple courses and each course can have multiple students. Which of the following data structures will be most suitable to print each course name in alphabetical order followed by name of students taking that course in alphabetical order.

a. TreeMap<String, List<String>>
b. TreeMap<String, HashSet<String>>
c. TreeMap<String, TreeSet<String>>
d. TreeMap<String, TreeMap<String, String>>

Ans: c

Answer Explanation:

TreeMap<String, TreeSet<String>> can be used to store a sorted list of course names along with a sorted set of student names.

TreeSet is a sorted collection without duplicates and can be used to store the names of students. The complexity for add and search operations for a TreeMap and a TreeSet is logarithmic.

1.6.2

The following data structure is suitable to save a phone book: city names in alphabetical order and the corresponding names of people in alphabetical order along with their phone numbers.

a. TreeMap<String, List<String>>
b. TreeMap<String, HashSet<String>>
c. TreeMap<String, TreeSet<String>>
d. TreeMap<String, TreeMap<String, String>>

Ans: d

Answer Explanation:

TreeMap<String, TreeMap<String, String>> can be used to store a sorted list of city names along with a sorted list of people names with their phone numbers.

The complexity for add and search operations for a TreeMap is logarithmic.

1.6.3

There are two HashMaps, first one can be used to search for phone numbers using first Name, the second one to get phone numbers by lastName. There can be multiple phone numbers for a firstName or lastName.

If a functionality needs to be provided to search for phone numbers using both first and last Name together, how can the search result using first two HashMaps be used:

a. provide intersection of first two results
b. provide union of first two results
c. all of the above
d. none of the above

Ans: a

Answer Explanation:

HashMap<String, String> hmap1;
HashMap<String, String> hmap2;

If there are two HashMaps, hmap1 that gives list of phone numbers for search using first Name and hmap2 that gives list of phone numbers for search using last Name. Intersection of these two lists will give the phone numbers for a given first and last Name.

list1.retailAll(list2)

The above retainAll() method will retain in list1 only the values that are in list2 thus keeping the intersection of the two lists.

1.6.4

The following data structure can be used to save millions of student names along with their scores, so that all students having score between 70 to 80 can be searched and printed

a. HashMap<Integer, String>
b. TreeMap<Integer, String>
c. HashMap<String, Integer>
d. TreeMap<String, Integer>

Ans: b

Answer Explanation:

TreeMap<Integer, String> can be used to store student scores in sorted order along with the student name. To find values of a specific range, treeMap.subMap(fromKey, toKey) can be used.

All students having score between 70 and 80 can be searched using treeMap.subMap(70, 80). subMap method returns a sorted Map with entries that have keys in the given range.

1.6.5

A movie theater has multiple shows with start and end time. To determine if the movie theater is free for a particular interval, all start times are added to treeSet1 and all end times are added to treeSet2.

Which of the following Tree set functions can be used to determine if there are no shows in a specified time interval.

a. subset
b. tailSet
c. headset
d. descendingSet

Ans: a

Answer Explanation:

The movie theater has multiple shows with start and end times. All the start times have been added to treeSet1 and all the end times have been added to treeSet2.

To determine if there are no shows for a given time interval between startTime and endTime, the subSet function can be used as follows:

treeSet1.subSet(startTime, endTime) – returns a Set containing all start times between the given time interval

treeSet2.subSet(startTime, endTime) – returns a Set containing all end times between the given time interval

If the two sets returned by the above functions are empty then the theater is free for the given time interval.

1.6.6

Which of the following data structures is most suitable for printing elements of a queue in reverse order

a. stack
b. linked list
c. array
d. binary tree

Ans: a

Answer Explanation:

Elements from the front of the queue can be retrieved with dequeue method and then pushed into the stack. Once this operation is completed for all elements in the queue, the last element of the queue will be on top of the stack.

Using pop on the stack, the elements can be printed in the reverse order.

1.6.7

If h is the height of a full binary tree, the number of leaf nodes in the full binary tree is

a. 2^h
b. $h/2$
c. $h*2$
d. h^2

Ans: a

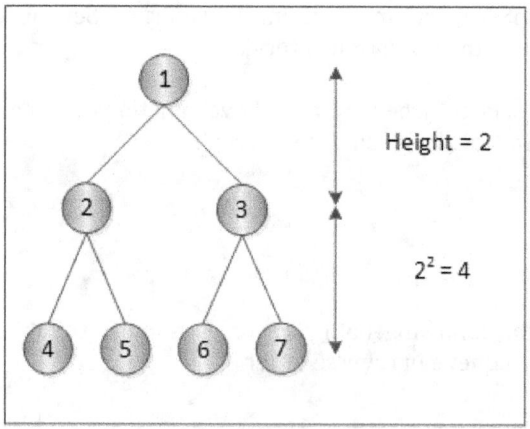

Answer Explanation:

Number of nodes when

h=0 is $2^0 = 1$
h=1 is $2^1 = 2$

h=2 is $2^2 = 4$

1.6.8

Which of the following sorts is most suitable for sorting large dataset on disk when there is a small amount of RAM to work with

a. merge sort
b. quick sort
c. heap sort
d. external merge sort

Ans: d

Answer Explanation:

Merge sort time complexity is $O(n \log n)$ and space complexity is $O(n)$. Merge sort uses divide and conquer method. Data is divided, sorted and then merged.

Merge sort can be used when data is huge but available memory is less. Data from the hard disk is loaded into the memory in chunks, sorted and then saved back to the disk in files. Once sorting is completed for the individual data chunks, they are merged. The sorted files are merged into larger files.

When data is large and is loaded into memory in chunks for sorting, it's called external sorting. For sorting individual data chunks, quick sort can be used as it's fast.

Also, since quick sort is an in place sort, doesn't take up extra memory. Then merge sort can be used to merge the individual sorted data in the files.

1.6.9

To find the largest 100 numbers out of 1 billion integers, which of the following data structures of size 100 can be used

a. min heap
b. binary tree
c. array
d. hash table

Ans: a

Answer Explanation:

Create a min heap of first hundred numbers. Compare the root node of min heap which is the minimum value with the next number in the unsorted input. If the input number is greater than the root value, replace the root with the input and continue this operation.

Finally, after comparing and adding all elements from the input, the last 100 values in the min heap will be the largest.

Min heap is an implementation of Priority Queue. Priority Queue supports insert and delete of min or max element in a data structure.

Algorithms

2.1 DYNAMIC PROGRAMMING

2.1.1

Given an array of integers, find the first index of a number that has sum left equals sum right.

Array {1, 3, 4, 2, 2} should return index as 2, as the sum of numbers to left of 4 and to it's right is the same.

To find the array balance index the left sum of the array can be compared with the right sum at each index. The left sum can be computed by adding each of the values starting from the left. Right sum can be computed using

a. left sum
b. total sum
c. total sum and left sum
d. none of the above

Ans: c

Answer Explanation:

Code:

```
public static int findFirstBalancedIndex(int [] arr) {

    int totalSum = 0;
    int leftSum = 0;

    for(int val : arr) {
        totalSum += val;
    }

    for(int i=0; i<arr.length; i++) {

        leftSum += arr[i];
        if((leftSum - arr[i]) == (totalSum-leftSum)) {
            return i;
        }
    }
```

```
        return -1;
}
```

Test Code:

```
public static void main(String [] args) {

        int [] arr = {1, 3, 4, 2, 2};

        System.out.println("The balance index in the array is " +
        findFirstBalancedIndex(arr));
}
```

Output:

The balance index in the array is 2

Complexity:

Time Complexity: O(n) Space Complexity: O(1)

Explanation:

totalSum is computed first by adding all the numbers in the array.

Next, for each element leftSum is computed by adding the current element to the leftSum.

leftSum-arr[i] gives the leftSum of the array not inclusive of the current element.

totalSum-leftSum gives the right sum not including the current element.

(leftSum - arr[i]) and (totalSum-leftSum) will be computed for each index as below:

totalSum = 12

i=0 >>>>>   arr[i] = 1, leftSum = 1, (leftSum – arr[i]) = 0, (totalSum-leftSum) = 11

i=1 >>>>>   arr[i] = 3, leftSum = 4, (leftSum – arr[i]) = 1, (totalSum-leftSum) = 8 i=2 >>>>>   arr[i] = 4, leftSum = 8, (leftSum – arr[i]) = 4, (totalSum-leftSum) = 4

So, leftSum = rightSum = 4 when i=2

Here leftSum is computed not including the current element.

2.1.2

Given an unsorted array of integers, find the length of the longest consecutive elements sequence.

Given [100, 4, 200, 1, 3, 2], the longest consecutive element sequence is [1, 2, 3, 4] and it's length is 4.

If HashSet is used for finding the longest consecutive element sequence length, the time complexity and space complexity will be

a. O(1) and O(log n)
b. O(n) and O(n)
c. O(log n) and O(n)
d. O(n) and O(n^2)

Ans: b

Answer Explanation:

Code:

```
public static int getMaxSequence(int [] arr) {

    int max = 1;

    HashSet<Integer> set = new HashSet<Integer>();

    for(int value : arr) {

        set.add(value);
    }
```

```java
    for(int value : arr) {
        int count = 1;
        int next = value +1;
        int prev = value-1;

        while(set.contains(next)) {

            set.remove(next);
            next += 1;
            count++;
        }
        while(set.contains(prev)) {

            set.remove(prev);
            prev -= 1;
            count++;
        }
        if(count > max) {
            max = count;
        }
    }
    return max;
}
```

Test Code:

```java
public static void main(String [] args) {

    int [] arr = {100, 4, 200, 1, 3, 2};

    System.out.println("Number of longest consecutive sequence in "
    + Arrays.toString(arr) + " is " + getMaxSequence(arr));
}
```

Output:

Number of longest consecutive sequence in [100, 4, 200, 1, 3, 2] is 4

Complexity:

Time Complexity: O(n) Space Complexity: O(n)

Explanation:

Add elements in the array to the HashSet.

Iterate through each element in the array.

For each number, check if the previous and next numbers are present in the array.

If previous or next number is present, increase the count and repeat the last step.

value=100 >>>>>
count = 1, next = 101, previous = 99
max = 1

value=4 >>>>>
count = 1, next = 5, previous = 3
count = 2, next = 5, previous = 2
count = 3, next = 5, previous = 1
count = 4, next = 5, previous = 0
max=4

2.1.3

Write a function that, given a list of integers (both positive and negative) returns the sum of the contiguous subsequence with maximum sum. Given the sequence {1, 2, -4, 1, 3, -2, 3, -1} should return 5.

The best time complexity for the above function implementation would be

a. O(n)
b. O(log n)
c. O(n log n)
d. O(n^2)

Ans: a

Answer Explanation:

Code:

```java
public static int subArrayLargestSum(int [] arr) {

    int max = 0;
    int maxSum = 0;

    for(int n : arr) {

        max += n;
        if(max < 0) {

            max = 0;
        }
        if(max > maxSum) {

            maxSum = max;
        }
    }
    return maxSum;
}
```

Test Code:

```java
public static void main(String [] args) {

    int [] arr = {1, 2, -4, 1, 3, -2, 3, -1};

    System.out.println("Largest    sum    of    subarray    "    +
    Arrays.toString(arr) + " is " + subArrayLargestSum(arr));
}
```

Output:

Largest sum of subarray [1, 2, -4, 1, 3, -2, 3, -1] is 5

Complexity:

Time Complexity: O(n) Space Complexity: O(1)

Explanation:

Iterate through each element in the array and add the number to variable 'max'. If 'max' is less than zero reset it to zero as we're not interested in sums less than zero. If max is greater than maxSum then set maxSum to max.

```
n=1  >>>>>   max=1, maxSum=1
n=2  >>>>>   max=3, maxSum=3
n=-4 >>>>>   max=0, maxSum=3
n=1  >>>>>   max=1, maxSum=3

n=3  >>>>>   max=4, maxSum=4
n=-2 >>>>>   max=2, maxSum=4
n=3  >>>>>   max=5, maxSum=5
n=-1 >>>>>   max=4, maxSum=5
```

2.2 STRING

2.2.1

Find if two strings passed are anagrams. For example 'post' and 'spot' should return true. If an HashSet is used for storing the characters of the first string, then time complexity and space complexity for implementing the above functionality will be

a. O(1) and O(log n)
b. O(n) and O(n)
c. O(log n) and O(n)
d. O(n) and O(n^2)

Ans: b

Answer Explanation:

Code:

```java
public static boolean isAnagram(String s1, String s2) {

    //str1 and str2 should have same length

    //add chars in s1 to HashMap map1 and s2 to map2 with
    //frequency and compare

    if(s1.length() != s2.length()) {

        return false;
    }

    HashMap<Character,    Integer>    map1    =    new
    HashMap<Character, Integer>();

    HashMap<Character,    Integer>    map2    =    new
    HashMap<Character, Integer>();

    //both strings are same length
```

```
        for(int i=0; i<s1.length(); i++) {

                char c1 = s1.charAt(i);
                char c2 = s2.charAt(i);

                if(map1.containsKey(c1)) {

                        map1.put(c1, map1.get(c1) +1);
                }
                else {
                        map1.put(c1, 1);
                }

                //repeat same for map2
                if(map2.containsKey(c2)) {

                        map2.put(c2, map2.get(c2) +1);
                }
                else {
                        map2.put(c2, 1);
                }
        }
        return map1.equals(map2);
}
```

Test Code:

```
public static void main(String [] args) {

    String s1 = "schoolmaster";
    String s2 = "theclassroom";

    System.out.println(s1 + ", " + s2 + " isAnagram " +
    isAnagram(s1, s2));
}
```

Output:

schoolmaster, theclassroom isAnagram true

Complexity:

Time Complexity: O(n) Space Complexity: O(n)

Explanation:

Check if both strings are of same length. If their lengths are equal then add all characters in str1 to the HashMap map1 and all characters in str2 to map2 with the frequency of occurrence for each character.

Check if both the hashmaps are equal to check if all characters with frequency of occurrence in map1 matches that of map2 to determine if the two strings are anagrams.

2.2.2

Implement a function to check if the input string passed is a palindrome. For example abcba and abba should return true, while abc should return false.

What would be the best time complexity for implementing this function?

a. O(1)
b. O(log n)
c. O(n)
d. O(n^2)

Ans: c

Answer Explanation:

Code:

```
public static boolean isPalindrome(String s) {

        char [] c = s.toCharArray();

        for(int i=0, j=c.length-1 ; i<j; i++, j--) {

                if(c[i] != c[j]) {
                        return false;
                }
        }
        return true;
```

```
}
```

Test Code:

```
public static void main(String [] args) {

    String [] arr = {"abcba", "abba", "abc", "aba", "aa", "a", ""};

    for(int i=0; i<arr.length; i++) {
        System.out.println(arr[i]+" "+Palindrome.isPalindrome(arr[i]));
    }
}
```

Output:

```
abcba true
abba true
abc false
aba true
aa true
a true
true
```

Complexity:

Time Complexity: O(n) Space Complexity: O(n)

Explanation:

Add contents of the string to a char array.

Iterate through the char array comparing first element with last, second element with last-1 and so on. If it's odd number of characters, the middle char is skipped.

```
s = abcba >>>>>
i = 0, j = 4, c[i] = a, c[j]=a
i = 1, j = 3, c[i] = b, c[j]=b
return true

s = abc >>>>>
i = 0, j = 2, c[i] = a, c[j]=c
return false
```

2.2.3

Implement a function that filters all letters passed to the constructor.

Filter filter = new Filter("AEIOU");
filter.apply("HELLO"); // filter all letters passed to constructor.
Should return HLL

What would be the best time complexity for implementing this function using a HashSet?

a. O(1)
b. O(log n)
c. O(n)
d. O(n^2)

Ans: c

Answer Explanation:

Code:

```
public class StringFilter {

    private String filter;

    public StringFilter(String filter) {

        this.filter = filter;
    }

    public String apply(String inputStr) {

        char [] output = new char[inputStr.length()];

        //Add filter to HashSet
        HashSet<Character> set = new HashSet<Character>();

        for(int i=0; i<filter.length(); i++) {

            set.add(filter.charAt(i));
        }
```

```
        //check if the input is present in hashset
        int j=0;

        for(int i=0; i<inputStr.length(); i++) {

            char ch = inputStr.charAt(i);

            if(!set.contains(ch)) {

                output[j++] = ch;
            }
        }

        return String.valueOf(output);
    }
}
```

Test Code:

```
public static void main(String [] args) {

    StringFilter fltr = new StringFilter("AEIOU");

    System.out.println("Filter   AEIOU   on   input   HELLO:   " +
    fltr.apply("HELLO"));
}
```

Output:

Filter AEIOU on input HELLO: HLL

Complexity:

Time Complexity: O(n) Space Complexity: O(n)

Explanation:

Add all characters in the filter to the HashSet.

Iterate through each character of the input string.

If the set does not contain the character from input string, add the character to the output char array.

Finally convert char array to String and return. Instead of char array, StringBuilder can be used to construct the output string from chars.

filter = AEIOU

inputStr = HELLO >>>>>
ch = H, output[0] = H
ch = E, output[0] = H

ch = L, output[1] = L
ch = L, output[2] = L
ch = O, output[2] = L

return HLL

2.2.4

Is input string x a substring of another string y.

String needle = "abc"
String haystack = "gfgghfjkabciggj"
should return 8, the beginning index of needle in the haystack.

The time complexity for implementing the above function is O(n), where n is the length of

a. needle
b. haystack
c. either
d. none of the above

Ans: b

Answer Explanation:

Code:

```
public static int subStringMatch(String haystack, String needle) {

    char [] hayChar = haystack.toCharArray();
```

```java
char [] needleChar = needle.toCharArray();

for(int j=0; j<hayChar.length; j++) {

    int count = 0;

    while((count < needleChar.length) &&
          (hayChar[j+count] == needleChar[count]))
    {
        count++;
    }

    if(count == needleChar.length) {

        return j;
    }
}

return -1;
}
```

Test Code:

```java
public static void main(String [] args) {

    String needle= "abc";

    String haystack = "gfgghfjkabciggj";

    System.out.println("abc matches gfgghfjkabciggj at index: "+
    subStringMatch(haystack, needle));
}
```

Output:

abc matches gfgghfjkabciggj at index: 8

Complexity:

Time Complexity: O(n) Space Complexity: O(n)

Explanation:

Add haystack and needle strings to char arrays.
Iterate through each character in haystack char array.

Check if there is a match for all characters of the needle inside haystack and return the begin index in haystack for this match.

needle = abc
haystack = gfgghfjkabciggj >>>>>
count = 0, j = 0, hayChar[j+count] = g, needleChar[count]=a
...
count = 0, j = 7, hayChar[j+count] = k, needleChar[count]=a
count = 0, j = 8, hayChar[j+count] = a, needleChar[count]=a

count = 1, j = 8, hayChar[j+count] = b, needleChar[count]=b
count = 2, j = 8, hayChar[j+count] = c, needleChar[count]=c

return 8

2.2.5

Write a function to reverse a string.

Input: abcdefg
Output: gfedcba

The best time complexity for reversing a string function is

a. O(1)
b. O(n)
c. O(n/2)
d. O(n^2)

Ans: c

Answer Explanation:

Code:

```
public static String reverse(String s) {

    char [] c = s.toCharArray();
```

```
    for(int i=0, j=c.length-1 ; i<j; i++, j--) {

        if(c[i] != c[j]) {

            //swap
            char temp = c[i];

            c[i] = c[j];
            c[j] = temp;
        }
    }
    return String.valueOf(c);
}

public static String reverseStr(String s) {

    StringBuilder rev = new StringBuilder();

    for(int i=s.length()-1; i>=0; i--) {

        rev.append(s.charAt(i));
    }
    return rev.toString();
}
```

Test Code:

```
public static void main(String [] args) {

    System.out.println(" abcdefg reverse: " + reverse("abcdefg"));

    System.out.println(" abcdefg reverseStr: " +
    reverseStr("abcdefg"));
}
```

Output:

abcdefg reverse: gfedcba
abcdefg reverseStr: gfedcba

Complexity:

Time Complexity: O(n) Space Complexity: O(n)

Explanation:

For reverse method, add contents of the string to a char array.

Iterate through the char array comparing first element with last, second element with last-1 and so on. If the chars are different swap them.

s = abcdefg >>>>>
i = 0, j = 6, c[i] = a, c[j]=g, swap
i = 1, j = 5, c[i] = b, c[j]=f, swap

i = 2, j = 4, c[i] = c, c[j]=e, swap
i = 3, j = 3, exit for loop

return gfedcba

2.2.6

Write a method for checking if the string follows a specific pattern

String ajhkjhkb9c should return true for following pattern a*b%c

The time complexity for a single pattern check in a string is O(n) where n is the length of

a. pattern in input
b. input
c. pattern
d. none of the above

Ans: a

Answer Explanation:

Code:

```
public static boolean findPatternMatch(String str, String pattern) {

        char [] patternChars = {'*', '%'};
```

```java
        for(char pChar: patternChars) {

            int index = pattern.indexOf(pChar);

            char beginChar = pattern.charAt(index-1);
            char endChar = pattern.charAt(index+1);

            if(findMatch(str, pChar, beginChar, endChar) == false)

                    return false;
        }
        return true;
}

public static boolean findMatch(String str, char patternChar,
                                char beginChar, char endChar) {

    int beginIndex = str.indexOf(beginChar);
    int endIndex = str.indexOf(endChar);

    if(patternChar == '*') {

        for(int i=beginIndex+1; i<endIndex; i++) {

            if(!Character.isDefined(str.charAt(i))) return false;
        }
    }
    else if(patternChar == '%') {

        for(int i=beginIndex+1; i<endIndex; i++) {

            if(!Character.isDigit(str.charAt(i))) return false;
        }
    }
    return true;
}
```

Test Code:

```java
public static void main(String [] args) {

    System.out.println("a*b%c pattern match for ajhkjhkb9c: " +
```

    findPatternMatch("ajhkjhkb9c", "a*b%c"));
}

Output:

a*b%c pattern match for ajhkjhkb9c: true

Complexity:

Time Complexity: O(n) Space Complexity: O(1)

Explanation:

For each pattern character like *and %, the begin and end characters in the pattern string are found and passed to the findMatch method. In the findMatch method, the begin and end index for the same characters in the input string are found.

All characters between the begin and end index in the input string are checked if they belong to the specific pattern. For example, * would be any character and % represents any number in this pattern check.

str=ajhkjhkb9c
pattern = a*b%c

pChar = * >>>>>
beginChar = a
endChar = b

beginIndex = 0
endIndex = 7
return true

pChar = % >>>>>
beginChar = b
endChar = c

beginIndex = 7
endIndex = 9
return true

2.2.7

Implement a function to find out the spaces between words when a sentence is typed.

For example if "I love airplane" is typed without spaces, solve to find out the spaces between words especially if a larger word has subset of words.

Assume a dictionary of words is passed as an argument. Different possible words for the input string can be constructed from

a. dictionary
b. input char array
c. all of the above
d. none of the above

Ans: b

Answer Explanation:

Code:

```java
public static String wordBreak(String input, Set<String> dictionary) {

    String output = "";
    String currentWord = "";

    HashMap<Integer, String> map =
        new HashMap<Integer, String>();

    int count=0;

    for(int i=0; i<input.length(); i++) {

        currentWord += input.charAt(i);

        if(dictionary.contains(map.get(count)+currentWord)) {

            String str = map.get(count)+currentWord;
            map.put(count, str);
            currentWord = "";
        }
```

```
        else if(dictionary.contains(currentWord)) {

                map.put(++count, currentWord);
                currentWord = "";
        }
    }

    for(int key : map.keySet()) {

            output += map.get(key) + " ";
    }
    return output;
}
```

Test Code:

```
public static void main(String [] args) {

    Set<String> dictionary = new HashSet<String>();
    dictionary.add("I");
    dictionary.add("love");
    dictionary.add("air");
    dictionary.add("plane");
    dictionary.add("airplane");

    System.out.println(wordBreak("Iloveairplane", dictionary));
}
```

Output:

I love airplane

Complexity:

Time Complexity: O(n) Space Complexity: O(n)

Explanation:

Iterate through each character in the input string and construct a word by appending one character at a time. Check if this constructed word has a match in the dictionary. If there is a match in the dictionary, add the word to a HashMap by incrementing the integer count as the key.

Prepend the last word in the HashMap with the constructed word and check if this new word is found in the dictionary. If there is a match in the dictionary, then replace the previous word stored in the HashMap with the new larger word.

Finally construct a sentence with the words stored in the HashMap.

input = Iloveairplane
currentWord = I >>>>>
map = 1:I
...
currentWord = love >>>>>
map = 1:I, 2:love
...
currentWord = air >>>>>
map = 1:I, 2:love, 3:air
...
currentWord = plane >>>>>
map = 1:I, 2:love, 3:airplane

return I love airplane

2.2.8

Implement a function to find the first character in a string which only appears once.

For example when the input is "abaccdeff" it should return b.

What would be the best time complexity for implementing this function using a HashSet to save the repeating chars and an ArrayList to save the non repeating chars?

a. O(1)
b. O(log n)
c. O(nlogn)
d. O(n)

Ans: d

Answer Explanation:

Code:

```java
public static char findUniqueCharInString(String str) {

    char uniqueChar = '0'; //initialize to some value

    ArrayList<Character> nonRepeat
        = new ArrayList<Character>();

    HashSet<Character> repeat = new HashSet<Character>();

    char [] arr = str.toCharArray();

    for(char c: arr) {

        if(nonRepeat.contains(c)) {

            nonRepeat.remove((Character) c);
            repeat.add(c);

        } else if(!repeat.contains(c)) {

            nonRepeat.add(c);
        }
    }

    if(nonRepeat.size()>0) {

        uniqueChar = nonRepeat.get(0);
    }
    return uniqueChar;
}
```

Test Code:

```java
public static void main(String [] args) {

    String str = "abadeff";
    char uniqueChar = findUniqueCharInString (str);

    System.out.println("Input string " + str + " first unique char is " +
    uniqueChar);
}
```

Output:

Input string abaccdeff first unique char is b

Complexity:

Time Complexity: O(n) Space Complexity: O(n)

Explanation:

Add contents of the string to a char array.

Iterate through the char array, if the nonRepeat ArrayList contains the character, then remove it from the nonRepeat and add it to the repeat HashSet. If the repeat HashSet does not contain the char, add it to the nonRepeat ArrayList.

Once done with all the chars, return the first element of the nonRepeat ArrayList

str = abadeff >>>>>
c = a, nonRepeat = a, repeat =
c = b, nonRepeat = a b, repeat =
c = a, nonRepeat = b, repeat = a
c = d, nonRepeat = b d, repeat = a
c = e, nonRepeat = b d e, repeat = a
c = f, nonRepeat = b d e f, repeat = a
c = f, nonRepeat = b d e, repeat = a f

return b

2.2.9

Find the longest palindromic substring in a given string.

To find all possible palindromic substrings in a given string, each character in the string can be checked if it is the ___ of the palindrome.

a. middle
b. start
c. end

d. none of the above

Ans: a

Answer Explanation:

Code:

```java
public static String getLongestPalindromicSubstring (String str) {

    String longPalind = "";
    //skip first and last characters for checking
    for(int i=1; i<str.length()-1; i++) {

        //middle index is a character
        String palind = isPalindrome(str, i, i);
        if(palind.length() > longPalind.length()) {
            longPalind = palind;
        }
        //middle index between two characters
        palind = isPalindrome(str, i, i+1);
        if(palind.length() > longPalind.length()) {
            longPalind = palind;
        }
    }
    return longPalind;
}
//given center with one or two indices
private static String isPalindrome(String str, int beginIndex,
                                            int endIndex)
{
    String palindrome = "";

    while(beginIndex >=0 && endIndex <str.length()
    && (str.charAt(beginIndex) == str.charAt(endIndex))) {

        beginIndex--;
        endIndex++;
    }
    palindrome = str.substring(beginIndex+1, endIndex);

    return palindrome;
}
```

Test Code:

```
public static void main(String [] args) {

    String str = "tgkayakgytabccba";

    System.out.println("Longest palindrome substring for " + str + "
    is " + getLongestPalindromicSubstring (str));
}
```

Output:

Longest palindrome substring for tgkayakgytabccba is gkayakg

Complexity:

Time Complexity: O(n) Space Complexity: O(1)

Explanation:

The isPalindrome method compares the characters in the string with beginIndex and endIndex as the middle indexes.

For a palindromic string with an even number of characters like 'ANNA' the beginIndex and endIndex are adjacent indexes which is 1 and 2.

For a palindromic string with an odd number of characters like 'KAYAK', the beginIndex and endIndex are the same which is 2.

The characters in the beginIndex and endIndex are compared. If they match, then beginIndex is decremented and endIndex is incremented.

The next set of chars are compared iteratively to determine if the string is a palindrome.

str = tgkayakgytabccba >>>>>
beginIndex = 1, endIndex = 1, match
beginIndex = 0, endIndex = 2, no match
beginIndex = 1, endIndex = 2, no match
...
beginIndex = 4, endIndex = 4, match
beginIndex = 3, endIndex = 5, match
beginIndex = 2, endIndex = 6, match

beginIndex = 1, endIndex = 7, match
beginIndex = 0, endIndex = 8, no match
beginIndex = 4, endIndex = 5, no match
...

2.2.10

Given a string, convert it to a palindrome with least number of insertions possible.

If the string is not a palindrome and if any of the substrings are also not palindromes, then the string can be converted to a palindrome by appending a second string to it. The second string is the

a. copy of the original string
b. reverse of the original string
c. either a copy or reverse
d. none of the above

Ans: b

Answer Explanation:

Code:

```java
public class StringToPalindrome {

    public static void main(String [] args) {

        String str = "tgkayakgytab";
        String palindrome = getLongestPalindromicSubstring(str);

        int palinIndexBegin = str.indexOf(palindrome);
        int palinIndexEnd = palinIndexBegin+ palindrome.length();

        String beginString = str.substring(0, palinIndexBegin);
        String endString = str.substring(palinIndexEnd, str.length());

        System.out.println("palindrome:  " + palindrome + "
        beginString: " + beginString + " endString: " + endString
```

```java
        String reversedBegin = ReverseString.reverse(beginString);
        String reversedEnd = ReverseString.reverse(endString);

        String finalPalindrome = reversedEnd + beginString +
        palindrome + reversedBegin + endString;

        System.out.println("finalPalindrome: " + finalPalindrome);
    }

public static String getLongestPalindromicSubstring (String str) {

        String longPalind = "";
        //skip first and last characters for checking
        for(int i=1; i<str.length()-1; i++) {

                //middle index is a character
                String palind = isPalindrome(str, i, i);
                if(palind.length() > longPalind.length()) {
                        longPalind = palind;
                }
                //middle index between two characters
                palind = isPalindrome(str, i, i+1);
                if(palind.length() > longPalind.length()) {
                        longPalind = palind;
                }
        }
        return longPalind;
}
//given center with one or two indices
private static String isPalindrome(String str, int beginIndex,
                                                int endIndex)
{

        String palindrome = "";

        while(beginIndex >=0 && endIndex <str.length()
        && (str.charAt(beginIndex) == str.charAt(endIndex))) {

                beginIndex--;
                endIndex++;
        }
        palindrome = str.substring(beginIndex+1, endIndex);
        return palindrome;
}
```

}

Output:

palindrome: gkayakg beginString: t endString: ytab
finalPalindrome: batytgkayakgtytab

Complexity:

Time Complexity: O(n) Space Complexity: O(n)

Explanation:

Find the longest palindromic substring. Take substrings before and after this string.

Reverse the front substring and add to the end of the palindrome. Then reverse the end substring and add to the beginning of the palindrome.

str = tgkayakgytab >>>>>
palindrome = gkayakg
beginString = t
endString = ytab

reversedBegin = t
reversedEnd = baty
finalPalindrome: batytgkayakgtytab

2.3 RECURSION

2.3.1

```
public static int factorialRecurse(int n) {

    if(n ==0)  return 1;

    return n * factorialRecurse(n-1);
}
```

The above function factorialRecurse computes recursively the factorial of a number n. Factorial of n is the product of all positive integers that are less than n. For example: 4! = 4*3*2*1

What is time complexity for the above factorialRecurse function?

a. O(1)
b. O(log n)
c. O(n)
d. O(n^2)

Ans: c

Answer Explanation:

Code:

```
public static int factorialRecurse(int n) {

    if(n ==0) return 1;

    return n * factorialRecurse(n-1);
}
public static int factLoop(int n) {

    int fact = n;
    while(n > 1) {

        fact = fact * --n;
    }
```

```java
    return fact;
}
```

Test Code:

```java
public static void main(String [] args) {

    int [] arr = {1, 2, 3, 4, 5};

    for(int i=0; i<arr.length; i++) {

        System.out.println("Factorial for " + arr[i] + " is " +
        factorialRecurse(arr[i]));
    }
}
```

Output:

Factorial for 1 is 1
Factorial for 2 is 2
Factorial for 3 is 6
Factorial for 4 is 24
Factorial for 5 is 120

Complexity:

Time Complexity: O(n) Space Complexity: O(1)

Explanation:

The function factorialRecurse is called recursively n times so the time complexity for this function is O(n).

2.3.2

Fibonacci sequence is computed by adding the previous two numbers. 1, 1, 2, 3, 5, 8, 13, 21, 34 and so on is a fibonacci series. The function fibonacciRecurse computes recursively the nth number in the fibonacci sequence.

```
public static int fibonacciRecurse(int n) {

    if(n<=1) return n;

    return fibonacciRecurse(n-1) + fibonacciRecurse(n-2);
}
```

What is time complexity for the above fibonacciRecurse function?

a. O(log n)
b. O(n)
c. O(n^2)
d. O(2^n)

Ans: d

Answer Explanation:

Code:

```
public static int fibonacciRecurse(int n) {

    if(n<=1)  return n;

    return fibonacciRecurse(n-1) + fibonacciRecurse(n-2);
}

public static int fibonacciLoop(int n) {

    if(n<=1)  return n;

    int n1 = 1;
    int n2 = 1;
    int n3 = 1;

    for(int i=3; i<=n; i++) {

        n3 = n1 + n2;
        n1 = n2;
        n2 = n3;
    }
    return n3;
}
```

Test Code:

```java
public static void main(String [] args) {

    int [] arr = {1, 2, 3, 4, 5, 6, 7};
    for(int i=0; i<arr.length; i++) {

        System.out.println("Fibonacci for " + arr[i] + " is " +
        fibonacciRecurse(arr[i]));
    }
}
```

Output:

Fibonacci for 1 is 1
Fibonacci for 2 is 1
Fibonacci for 3 is 2
Fibonacci for 4 is 3
Fibonacci for 5 is 5
Fibonacci for 6 is 8
Fibonacci for 7 is 13

Complexity:

Recursion:
Time Complexity: $O(2^n)$ Space Complexity: $O(1)$
Loop:
Time Complexity: $O(n)$ Space Complexity: $O(1)$

Explanation:

The function fibonacciRecurse calls itself twice recursively, so the time complexity for this function is exponential or $O(2^n)$.

2.3.3

```java
public static String reverseString(String str) {

    if(str.length() <= 1) { return str; }

    return reverseString(str.substring(1)) + str.charAt(0);
```

}

public static void main(String [] args) {

    System.*out*println(reverseString("abc"));
}

The above program will print

a. abc
b. cba
c. bac
d. bca

Ans: b

Answer Explanation:

Code:

public static String reverseString(String str) {

    if(str.length() <= 1) { **return** str; }

    return reverseString(str.substring(1)) + str.charAt(0);
}

Test Code:

public static void main(String [] args) {

    String str = "abc";
    System.*out*println("Reverse of " + str + " is " +
    reverseString(str));
}

Output:

Reverse of abc is cba

Complexity:

Time Complexity: O(n) Space Complexity: O(1)

Explanation:

Each call of the recursion function reverseString appends the first character of the string to the end and calls the function with rest of the characters (not including the first character).

str = abc >>>>>
reverseString(abc)>>calls>>reverseString(bc)>>calls>> reverseString(c)

reverseString(c) returns c
reverseString(bc) returns cb
reverseString(abc) returns cba

2.3.4

```java
public class RecursionVariable {

    private static class Entry {

        String value;
        Entry parent;

        public Entry(String val) {
            value = val;
            parent = null;
        }
    }

    public static void printParentFirst(Entry e) {

        if(e!= null && e.parent != null) {

            printParentFirst(e.parent);
        }
        if(e!= null) {

            System.out.print(e.value);
        }
    }
```

```java
public static void main(String [] args) {

        Entry e3 = new Entry("3");
        Entry e2 = new Entry("2");
        Entry e1 = new Entry("1");
        e3.parent = e2;
        e3.parent.parent = e1;

        printParentFirst(e3);
    }
}
```

The above program will print

a. 123
b. 321
c. 231
d. none of the above

Ans: a

Answer Explanation:

Code:

```java
public class RecursionVariable {

    //prints parent first and stops if circular list
    public static void printParentFirstAndStopIfCircularList(Entry e) {

        if( e!= null && e.parent != null) {

            printParentFirstAndStop(e.parent, e);
        }
        if(e!= null) {
            System.out.print(e.value);
        }
    }

    public static void printParentFirstAndStop(Entry e, Entry first) {

        if( e!= null && e.parent != null && e!= first ) {
```

```
            printParentFirstAndStop(e.parent, first);
        }
        if( e!= null && e!= first) {
            System.out.print(e.value);
        }
    }
}
```

Test Code:

```
public static void main(String [] args) {

    Entry e3 = new Entry("3");
    Entry e2 = new Entry("2");
    Entry e1 = new Entry("1");
    e3.parent = e2;
    e3.parent.parent = e1;

    printParentFirst(e3);
}
```

Output:

123

Test Code:

```
public static void main(String [] args) {

    Entry e3 = new Entry("3");
    Entry e2 = new Entry("2");
    Entry e1 = new Entry("1");

    e3.parent = e2;
    e3.parent.parent = e1;
    e1.parent = e3; //circular list

    System.out.print("printParentFirstAndStopIfCircularList: ");
    printParentFirstAndStopIfCircularList(e3);
}
```

Output:

printParentFirstAndStopIfCircularList: 123

Complexity:

Time Complexity: O(n) Space Complexity: O(1)

Explanation:

Each Entry has a parent and the printParentFirst method recursively prints the top parent in the list whose parent is null followed by all children.

printParentFirstAndStopIfCircularList method has same functionality as printParentFirst method, but also checks if it's a circular list. If circular list, this method stops printing the list.

e = e3 >>>>>
printParentFirst(e3) >>calls>> printParentFirst(e2) >>calls>> printParentFirst(e1)

printParentFirst(e1) prints 1
printParentFirst(e2) prints 2
printParentFirst(e3) prints 3

2.4 NUMBER

2.4.1

An array of 100 integers containing numbers 1 to 100 is shuffled and one number is removed.

What is the best time complexity for finding the missing number?

a. O(1)
b. O(log n)
c. O(n)
d. O(n^2)

Ans: c

Answer Explanation:

Find the sum for 100 numbers using, sum= n*(n+1)/2

Find sum of all integers in the given array. Difference between the two sums will give the missing number.

Time Complexity: O(n) Space Complexity: O(1)

Other solutions:

1. For each number from 1 to 100, check if the number is in the array
- Time complexity O(n^2), Space complexity O(1)

2. Sort the list and find the missing number in contiguous element
- Time complexity O(nlogn), Space complexity O(1)

3. Add all numbers to a HashSet and iterate through the array and find the missing value.
- Time complexity O(n), Space complexity O(n)

Code:

```
public static int getMissingInteger(Integer [] arr) {

        int n = arr.length + 1;     //+1 for missing number
```

```
    int sum = n * (n+1)/2;

    int arrSum = 0;

    for(int i=0; i< arr.length; i++) {
        arrSum += arr[i];
    }
    return sum - arrSum;
}
```

Test Code:

```
public static void main(String [] args) {

    ArrayList<Integer> list = new ArrayList<Integer>();

    for(int i=1; i<=100; i++) {
        list.add(i);
    }
    //remove number 17 from index 16
    list.remove(16);

    //shuffle and add list to array
    Collections.shuffle(list);
    Integer [] arr = new Integer[list.size()];

    System.out.println("MissingInteger is " +
    getMissingInteger(list.toArray(arr)));
}
```

Output:

MissingInteger is 17

Complexity:

Time Complexity: O(n) Space Complexity: O(1)

Explanation:

Numbers 1 to 100 are added to an ArrayList. Number 17 is removed from the list and the list is shuffled using Collections.shuffle() method. Contents of this list are added to an array using list.toArray()

method. The array is passed to the getMissingInteger method which returns number 17.

In the getMissingInteger() method, sum of 1 to 100 is computed using, sum= n*(n+1)/2. Sum of the array with missing integer arrSum is computed by iterating through the array. Difference between the sum of 100 integers and the arrSum gives the missing number which is 17.

2.4.2

The time complexity for reversing a positive integer is

a. O(1)
b. O(log n)
c. O(n)
d. O(n^2)

Ans: c

Answer Explanation:

The time complexity for reversing an integer is O(n) where n is the number of digits.

Code:

```
public static int reverseInteger(int value) {

    if (value <= 0) { return value; }

    int reverse = 0;
    int exp = 1;

    while((value/exp) > 0) {

        int lastDigit = (value/exp) %10;
        reverse = (reverse *10) + lastDigit;
        exp = exp * 10;
    }
    return reverse;
}
```

Test Code:

```
public static void main (String [] args) {

    int num = 1234;
    System.outprintln("Reverse of " + num + " is: " +
    reverseInteger(num));
}
```

Output:

Reverse of 1234 is: 4321

Complexity:

Time Complexity: O(n) Space Complexity: O(1)

Explanation:

The last digit of the number is extracted by computing the number % 10, modulo operator gives the remainder of the number after dividing by 10.

Last digit extracted is saved to variable 'reverse'. This operation is continued after dividing the input number with 10, 100, 1000 and so on till all the digits are extracted and added to the 'reverse' variable.

value = 1234 >>>>>
exp = 1, lastDigit = 4, reverse = 4
exp = 10, lastDigit = 3, reverse = 43
exp = 100, lastDigit = 2, reverse = 432
exp = 1000, lastDigit = 1, reverse = 4321

return 4321

2.4.3

What is the time complexity for converting an integer to String without using java utility functions?

For example integer 1234 should return String "1234". Individual numbers 1 2 3 4 can be added into an array list and then converted to a string.

a. O(1)
b. O(log n)
c. O(n)
d. O(n^2)

Ans: c

Answer Explanation:

Time complexity for converting an integer to String is O(n) where n is the number of digits.

Code:

```
public static String convertIntToString(int n) {

    if(n ==0) { return "0"; }

    boolean isNegative = false;

    if(n < 0) {
        //set flag and make number positive
        isNegative = true;
        n = Math.abs(n);
    }

    //take digits from LSD and add to array list
    int exp=1;
    ArrayList<Integer> numList = new ArrayList<Integer>();

    while((n/exp) != 0) {

        int lastDigit = (n/exp)%10;
        numList.add(lastDigit);
        exp = exp*10;
    }

    //since digits were taken from LSD, need to reverse array list
    Collections.reverse(numList);
```

```
    StringBuilder sb = new StringBuilder();

    if(isNegative) {
        sb.append("-");
    }
    for(int num : numList) {
        char c = (char) ('0' + num);
        sb.append(c);
    }
    return sb.toString();
}
```

Test Code:

```
public static void main(String [] args) {

    System.out.println("Convert -1234 to string: " +
    convertIntToString(-1234));
}
```

Output:

Convert -1234 to string: -1234

Complexity:

Time Complexity: O(n) Space Complexity: O(1)

Explanation:

The last digit of the number is extracted by computing the input number % 10, modulo operator gives the remainder of the number after dividing by 10.

Last digit extracted is saved to numList which is an array list. Since the digits are taken from LSD (Least Significant Digit), the numList is reversed using Collections.reverse() method.

Iterate through the numbers in numList and append them to a StringBuilder to finally convert it to a String.

Since this is a negative number, the isNegative flag is set to true and the number is made positive using Math.abs() method. Finally minus sign is added to the output StringBuilder if the isNegative flag is true.

n = -1234
isNegative = true

n = 1234 >>>>>
exp = 1, lastDigit = 4, numList = 4
exp = 10, lastDigit = 3, numList = 43
exp = 100, lastDigit = 2, numList = 432
exp = 1000, lastDigit = 1, numList = 4321

numList = 1234

return -1234

2.4.4

What is the time complexity for finding the square root of a number?

a. O(1)
b. O(log n)
c. O(n)
d. O(n^2)

Ans: b

Answer Explanation:

Time complexity for finding the square root of a number is O(log n) as modified binarySearch can be used.

Code:

```
public static int findSquareRoot(int n) {

    if(n<=1) return n;

    int start =0;
    int end = n;

    while(start < end) {
```

```
        int mid = (start+end)/2;

        if(mid*mid == n) return mid;

        if(mid*mid > n) {

                end = mid-1;
        }
        else {
                start = mid+1;
        }
    }
    return Math.min(start, end);
}
```

Test Code:

```
public static void main(String [] args) {

        System.out.println( "Square root of 100 is: " +
        findSquareRoot(100));
}
```

Output:

Square root of 100 is: 10

Complexity:

Time Complexity: O(log n) Space Complexity: O(1)

Explanation:

To find square root of a number n, variable 'start' is initialized to zero and 'end' to n. Variable 'mid' is computed using (start+end)/2.

If square of mid is larger than n, then mid has to be a smaller number and end is set to mid-1, shifting to first half of the range. Similarly if square of mid is smaller than n, then mid has to be a larger number, so start is set to mid+1, shifting to the second half.

This iteration is continued till square of mid equals n and the mid value is returned. At the end of the iteration, if 'start' is greater than or equal to 'end' then, smaller of the two values is returned.

n = 100 >>>>>
start = 0, end = 100, mid = 50
start = 0, end = 49, mid = 24
start = 0, end = 23, mid = 11

start = 0, end = 10, mid = 5
start = 6, end = 10, mid = 8
start = 9, end = 10, mid = 9
start = 10, end = 10

return 10

2.5 SEARCH

2.5.1

```java
public static int binarySearch(int [] arr, int target) {

    int start = 0;
    int end = arr.length - 1;
    int mid;

    while (start <= end) {

        mid = (start + end) / 2;

        if( arr[mid] < target ) {

            start = mid + 1;
        }
        else if( arr[mid] > target) {

            end = mid - 1;
        }
        else {
            return mid;
        }
    }
    return -1;
}

public static void main(String [] args) {

    int [] a = {1,2,3,4,5,6,7};

    for(int i=1; i<=7; i++) {
        System.out.println("Index of "+i+" is "+ binarySearch(a,i));
    }
}
```

For the above program, when i=5, BinarySearch.*search*(a, i) returns an index value of

a. 2

b. 3
c. 4
d. 5

Ans: c

Answer Explanation:

Output:

Index of 1 is 0
Index of 2 is 1
Index of 3 is 2
Index of 4 is 3
Index of 5 is 4
Index of 6 is 5
Index of 7 is 6

Complexity:

Time Complexity: O(log n) Space Complexity: O(1)

Explanation:

The binarySearch() method checks if an input number 'target' exists in an input array of numbers sorted in ascending order. For binarySearch to work, the input array should be sorted.

Variable 'start' is initialized to zero and 'end' to length of the array. Variable 'mid' is computed using (start+end)/2. If arr[mid] is less than the target, second half of the array needs to be searched, so 'start' is set to mid+1.

Similarly, if arr[mid] is more than the target, first half of the array needs to be searched, so 'end' is set to mid-1.

If the arr[mid] value matches the target, then index 'mid' is returned.

2.5.2

Given two integer arrays, find the intersection of the two.

Eg: arr1 = {1,3,6,10}, arr2 = {2,3,5,6} the function should return {3,6}

What is the time complexity for implementing the above functionality using a HashSet?

a. O(1)
b. O(log n)
c. O(n)
d. O(n^2)

Ans: c

Answer Explanation:

Code:

```
public static int [] arrayIntersect(int [] a, int [] b) {

    HashSet<Integer> set = new HashSet<Integer>();

    for(int i : a) { set.add(i); }

    int [] output = new int [set.size()];
    int k =0;

    for(int val : b) {

        if(set.contains(val)) {
            output[k++] = val;
        }
    }
    return output;
}
```

Test Code:

```
public static void main (String [] args) {

    int [] arr1 = {1,3,6,10};
    int [] arr2 = {2,3,5,6};

    System.out.println("Intersection of " + Arrays.toString(arr1)+ "
    and " + Arrays.toString(arr2) + " is " +
```

```
        Arrays.toString(arrayIntersect(arr1, arr2)));
}
```

Output:

Intersection of [1, 3, 6, 10] and [2, 3, 5, 6] is [3, 6, 0, 0]

Complexity:

Time Complexity: O(n) Space Complexity: O(n)

Explanation:

The arrayIntersect method takes two input arrays a and b.

Add contents of array a to the HashSet. Iterate through numbers in array b. If the set contains the number from array b, add the number to the output array.

```
a = [1, 3, 6, 10]
b = [2, 3, 5, 6] >>>>>

val = 2, arr = [0, 0, 0, 0]
val = 3, arr = [3, 0, 0, 0]
val = 5, arr = [3, 0, 0, 0]
val = 6, arr = [3, 6, 0, 0]
return [3, 6, 0, 0]
```

2.5.3

Find the local min in an array. An element is a local min if it's less than or equal to it's neighbors.

If a[mid-1] >= a[mid] and a[mid+1] >= a[mid] , then a[mid] is a local minimum.

Local min in an array can be determined by using the following:

a. binary search
b. recursion
c. binary tree

d. stack

Ans: a

Answer Explanation:

Code:

```
public static int arrayLocalMin(int [] arr, int low, int high) {

    if(low>high) return -1;

    int mid = (low+high)/2;

    if (arr[mid-1] >= arr[mid] && arr[mid+1] >= arr[mid]) {
        return arr[mid];
    }
    else if(arr[mid-1] <=arr[mid]) {

        return arrayLocalMin(arr, low, mid);
    }
    else {
        return arrayLocalMin(arr, mid, high);
    }
}
```

Test Code:

```
public static void main(String [] args) {

    int [] arr = {8,2,4,9,6,7,3,4};

    System.out.println("Local minimum value is " +
    arrayLocalMin(arr, 0, arr.length-1));
}
```

Output:

Local minimum value is 2

Complexity:

Time Complexity: O(log n) Space Complexity: O(1)

Explanation:

To find local min of an array, variable 'low' is set to zero and 'high' to array length. 'mid' is computed using (low+high)/2. If arr[mid-1] >= arr[mid] and arr[mid+1] >= arr[mid] , then arr[mid] is a local minimum.

If arr[mid-1] <= arr[mid], shift search to the left half of the array by setting high to mid, otherwise shift search to right half of the array by setting low to mid and search recursively.

arr = [8,2,4,9,6,7,3,4] >>>>>
low = 0, high = 7, mid = 3
low = 0, high = 3, mid = 1
arr[mid] = 2

return 2

2.5.4

To find the number that appears maximum number of times in an array, following would be the method with the best time complexity.

a. Compare each element with all other elements to find count and then max count of all elements.
b. After sorting, find if adjacent elements are repeated.
c. Add each number to a HashMap key and the number of occurrences as value.
d. None of the above.

Ans: c

Answer Explanation:

Following are the few ways to implement the functionality to find the number that occurs maximum number of times in an array.

1. Compare each element with all other elements to find the count, then find max count of all elements.
- Time complexity O(n^2) Space complexity O(1)

2. Sort the array and find if the adjacent elements are repeated.
- Time complexity O(nlogn) Space complexity O(1)

3. Add each number as a HashMap key and the number of occurrences as value.
- Time complexity O(n) Space complexity O(n)

Code:

```java
public static int arrayMaxOccurrence(int [] arr) {

    HashMap<Integer, Integer> map =
        new HashMap<Integer, Integer>();

    for(int i=0; i<arr.length; i++) {

        Integer count = map.get(arr[i]);

        if(count == null) {
            map.put(arr[i], 1);
        }
        else {
            map.put(arr[i], count+1);
        }
    }
    Integer max = Collections.max(map.values());

    return max;
}
```

Test Code:

```java
public static void main(String [] args) {

    int [] arr = {1,4,1,8,8,4,8,8,8};

    System.out.println("Max occurrence is "
    + arrayMaxOccurrence(arr));
}
```

Output:

Max occurrence is 5

Complexity:

Time Complexity: O(n) Space Complexity: O(n)

Explanation:

Iterate through the array and add each number into the HashMap as key. When a number has been saved to the HashMap already, map.get(arr[i]) returns the count, which is incremented and then added as value for this key.

map.get(arr[i]) returns null when the key is being added for the first time and the value is set as 1.

After iterating through all elements of the array and adding to the HashMap, the max value can be found using the function Collections.*max*(map.values()).

arr = [1,4,1,8,8,4,8,8,8] >>>>>
i=0, arr[i]=1, count=null, map=1:1
i=1, arr[i]=4, count=null, map=1:1, 4:1
i=2, arr[i]=1, count=1, map=   1:2, 4:1

i=3, arr[i]=8, count=null, map=1:2, 4:1, 8:1
i=4, arr[i]=8, count=1, map=   1:2, 4:1, 8:2
i=5, arr[i]=4, count=1, map=   1:2, 4:2, 8:2

i=6, arr[i]=8, count=2, map=   1:2, 4:2, 8:3
i=7, arr[i]=8, count=3, map=   1:2, 4:2, 8:4
i=8, arr[i]=8, count=4, map=   1:2, 4:2, 8:5

return 5

2.5.5

For an unsorted array of integers, each integer appears twice except one integer which appears once.

Write a function to find the integer that appears only once.

What is the time and space complexity for implementing the above function using a HashSet?

a. O(n^2) and O(n)
b. O(1) and O(n)
c. O(log n) and O(1)
d. O(n) and O(n)

Ans: d

Answer Explanation:

Code:

```java
public static int arrayNonRepeatingInteger(int [] arr) {

    int result = -1;
    HashSet<Integer> set = new HashSet<Integer>();

    for(int i : arr) {

        if(set.contains(i)) {
            set.remove(i);
        }
        else {
            set.add(i);
        }
    }

    if(set.size() >= 1) {
        result = set.iterator().next();
    }
    return result;
}
```

Test Code:

```java
public static void main(String [] args) {

    int [] arr = {1,2,4,5,4,2,1,8,8};
    System.out.println("Non repeating integer is " +
    arrayNonRepeatingInteger(arr));
}
```

Output:

Non repeating integer is 5

Complexity:

Time Complexity: O(n) Space Complexity: O(n)

Explanation:

Iterate through the numbers in the array.

Add each number in the array into a HashSet. If the HashSet already contains the number, remove the number. If the number is not present in the HashSet, add the number.

Finally the set will contain the non repeating number that is returned.

```
arr = [1,2,4,5,4,2,1,8,8] >>>>>
i = 0, arr[i] = 1, set = 1
i = 1, arr[i] = 2, set = 1,2
i = 2, arr[i] = 4, set = 1,2,4
i = 3, arr[i] = 5, set = 1,2,4,5

i = 4, arr[i] = 4, set = 1,2,5
i = 5, arr[i] = 2, set = 1,5
i = 6, arr[i] = 1, set = 5
i = 7, arr[i] = 8, set = 5,8
i = 8, arr[i] = 8, set = 5

return 5
```

2.5.6

Given an array of integers, find a pair with a given sum.

Eg: For array {1,2,4,5,6,7,8} and a given sum 15, there exists a pair 7 and 8.

What is the time complexity for implementing the above functionality using a HashSet?

a. O(1)
b. O(log n)
c. O(n)
d. O(n^2)

Ans: c

Answer Explanation:

Code:

```java
public static String findArrayPairForSum(int [] arr, int sum) {

    String result = "";
    HashSet<Integer> set= new HashSet<Integer>();

    for(int a : arr) {
        set.add(a);
    }

    for(int a : arr) {
        set.remove(a);
        int value = sum - a;

        if(value >0 && set.contains(value)) {

            result = a + ", " + value;
            return result;
        }
    }
    return result;
}
```

Test Code:

```java
public static void main(String [] args) {

    int [] arr = {1,2,4,5,6,7,8};
    int sum = 15;

    System.out.println("Pair with sum " + sum + " is " +
    findArrayPairForSum(arr, sum));
}
```

Output:

Pair with sum 15 is 7, 8

Complexity:

Time Complexity: O(n) Space Complexity: O(n)

Explanation:

Add contents of the array into a HashSet. Iterate through the numbers in the array.

Remove the number from the set, so it's not reused. To get the second number for the sum, compute the difference between the sum and the number.

Check if the second number is present in the set, if it does, return the two values.

sum=15
arr = [1,2,4,5,6,7,8] >>>>>

a = 1, value = 14
a = 2, value = 13
a = 4, value = 11
a = 5, value = 10
a = 6, value = 9
a = 7, value = 8
return 7,8

2.5.7

Search for a given target in a rotated array.

Eg: For array {5,6,7,1,2,3,4} return index of the target.

What is the time complexity for implementing the above functionality?

a. O(1)
b. O(log n)

c. O(n)
d. O(n^2)

Ans: b

Answer Explanation:

Code:

```java
public static int rotatedArraySearch(int [] arr, int target, int start,
                                                            int end)
{
    if(start > end) return -1;

    int mid = (start+end)/2;

    if(arr[mid] == target) {
        return mid;
    }

    if(arr[start] <= arr[mid]) {

        if(target >= arr[start] && target < arr[mid]) {

            end = mid-1;
        }
        else {
            start = mid+1;
        }
        return rotatedArraySearch(arr, target, start, end);
    }
    else {
        if(target > arr[mid] && target <= arr[end]) {

            start = mid+1;
        }
        else {
            end = mid-1;
        }
        return rotatedArraySearch(arr, target, start, end);
    }
}
```

Test Code:

```
public static void main(String [] args) {

    int target = 7;

    System.out.println("Index for value: " + target + " is " +
    rotatedArraySearch(arr, target, 0, arr.length-1));
}
```

Output:

Index for value: 7 is 2

Complexity:

Time Complexity: O(log n) Space Complexity: O(1)

Explanation:

Variable 'start' is set to zero and 'end' to array length. 'mid' is computed using (start+end)/2.

If arr[start] <= arr[mid], then the first half of the array is in ascending order, so start the search in this half.

If the target is between 'start' and 'mid', then target is in the left half, set end=mid-1, otherwise search the right half by setting start = mid+1.

If the first half of the array was not in ascending order, start search in the second half.

If target is between mid and end, set start=mid+1 otherwise set end=mid-1 and search recursively.

target = 7 >>>>>

start = 0 end = 6 mid = 3
start = 0 end = 2 mid = 1
start = 2 end = 2 mid = 2

return 2

2.5.8

Given a sorted array with duplicate values, find the start and end index of a target value.

Given [2,3,5,5,5,7,8,9,9,9] and target 5 should return [2,4] and target 4 should return [-1,-1]

Start and end index of a target can be found using:

a. HashSet
b. recursion
c. binary tree
d. binary search

Ans: d

Answer Explanation:

Code:

```
public static int [] findTargetRange(int [] arr, int target) {

    int [] result = {-1,-1};

    int low = findTargetFirstIndex(arr, target, 0, arr.length-1);

    if(low >= arr.length || arr[low] != target) return result;

    int high = findTargetLastIndex(arr, target, 0, arr.length-1);

    result[0] = low;
    result[1] = high;

    return result;
}

public static int findTargetFirstIndex(int [] arr, int target, int start,
                                                            int end)
{
    if(start>end) return -1;

    int mid = (start+end)/2;
```

```java
if(arr[mid] == target && (arr[mid-1]<target || mid==0)) {

        return mid;
    }
    else if(target > arr[mid]) {

        return findTargetFirstIndex(arr, target, mid+1, end);
    }
    else {
        return findTargetFirstIndex(arr, target, start, mid-1);
    }
}

public static int findTargetLastIndex(int [] arr, int target, int start,
                                                        int end)
{
    if(start>end) return -1;

    int mid = (start+end)/2;

    if(arr[mid] == target &&
      (arr[mid+1]>target || mid==arr.length-1))
    {
        return mid;
    }
    else if(target > arr[mid]) {

        return findTargetLastIndex(arr, target, mid+1, end);
    }
    else {
        return findTargetLastIndex(arr, target, start, mid-1);
    }
}
```

Test Code:

```java
public static void main(String [] args) {

    int [] arr = {2,3,5,5,5,7,8,9,9,9};

    int [] result = findTargetRange(arr, 5);
```

```
    System.out.println("Range for target 5 is " +
    Arrays.toString(result));
}
```

Output:

Range for target 5 is [2, 4]

Complexity:

Time Complexity: O(log n) Space Complexity: O(1)

Explanation:

Variable 'start' is set to zero and 'end' to array length. 'mid' is computed using (start+end)/2.

To find the first index of the target, check if arr[mid] matches the target. Also check if the number to the left is less than the target or if the target is the first element in the array.

Similarly, to find the last index of the target, check if arr[mid] matches the target, then check if the number to the right is greater than the target or if the target is the last element in the array.

If the target is greater than arr[mid], search in the right half of the array, otherwise search in the left half recursively.

arr = [2,3,5,5,5,7,8,9,9,9]

findTargetFirstIndex
target = 5 >>>>>

start = 0 end = 9 mid = 4
start = 0 end = 3 mid = 1
start = 2 end = 3 mid = 2
return 2

findTargetLastIndex
target = 5 >>>>>

start = 0 end = 9 mid = 4
return 4

2.5.9

Print the repeating numbers in an array, [10, 5, 3, 4, 3, 5, 6] should print 5 and 3.

What is the time and space complexity for implementing the above function using a HashSet?

a. O(n^2) and O(n)
b. O(n) and O(n)
c. O(log n) and O(1)
d. O(n) and O(1)

Ans: b

Answer Explanation:

Code:

```java
public static void findRepeatingNumber(int [] arr) {

    HashSet<Integer> set = new HashSet<Integer>();

    System.out.println("Repeating numbers: ");

    for(int n : arr) {

        if(set.add(n) == false) {

            System.out.print( n + " " );
        }
    }
}
```

Test Code:

```java
public static void main(String [] args) {

    int [] arr = {10, 5, 3, 4, 3, 5, 6};

    findRepeatingNumber(arr);
}
```

Output:

Repeating numbers:
3 5

Complexity:

Time Complexity: O(n) Space Complexity: O(n)

Explanation:

Iterate through the numbers in the array.

Add each number in the array into a HashSet. If the HashSet already contains the number, print the number.

2.6 SORT

2.6.1

```java
public static void insertionSort(int [] arr) {

    for(int j=1; j<arr.length; j++) {

        int temp = arr[j];
        int i= j;

        while(i>0 && temp < arr[i-1]) {

            arr[i] = arr[i-1];
            i--;
        }
        arr[i] = temp;

        System.out.println("value of j: " + j + " " +
        Arrays.toString(arr));
    }
}

public static void main (String [] args) {

    int [] arr = {10, 4, 7, 2, 3};

    System.out.println("before sort: " + Arrays.toString(arr));
    insertionSort(arr);
    System.out.println("after sort: " + Arrays.toString(arr));
}
```

Output:

before sort: [10, 4, 7, 2, 3]

value of j: 1 [4, 10, 7, 2, 3]
value of j: 2 [4, 7, 10, 2, 3]
value of j: 3 [2, 4, 7, 10, 3]
value of j: 4 [2, 3, 4, 7, 10]

after sort: [2, 3, 4, 7, 10]

In the above implementation of insertion sort algorithm

a. Each value is compared with the next one and then swapped.
b. Each value is swapped with the minimum of rest of the values.
c. Each value is compared to all the previous ones till it's position is determined.
d. None of the above.

Ans: c

Answer Explanation:

Complexity:

Time Complexity: O(n^2) Space Complexity: O(n)

Explanation:

In the insertion sort algorithm, each value is compared with all the previous values. If the value is lesser than the previous value, then the previous value is moved one position to the right.

This comparison and swapping is continued till the value is greater than one of the previous values. If the value is greater than the previous value, then it's added to the next index of the previous value.

Complexity of insertion sort is O(n^2) which makes this not a likely option while sorting large number of items. Insertion sort is easy to implement but slow compared to merge sort, quick sort and heap sort.

arr = [10, 4, 7, 2, 3]

insertionSort >>>>>
j = 1, temp = 4 >>
i = 1, arr = [10, 10, 7, 2, 3]
i = 0, arr = [4, 10, 7, 2, 3]

j = 2, temp = 7 >>
i = 2, arr = [4, 10, 10, 2, 3]
i = 1, arr = [4, 7, 10, 2, 3]

j = 3, temp = 2 >>
i = 3, arr = [4, 7, 10, 10, 3]

i = 2, arr = [4, 7, 7, 10, 3]
i = 1, arr = [4, 4, 7, 10, 3]
i = 0, arr = [2, 4, 7, 10, 3]

j = 4, temp = 3 >>
i = 4, arr = [2, 4, 7, 10, 10]
i = 3, arr = [2, 4, 7, 7, 10]
i = 2, arr = [2, 4, 4, 7, 10]
i = 1, arr = [2, 3, 4, 7, 10]

2.6.2

```java
public class QuickSort {

    private int [] inputArr;

    public void sort(int [] input) {

        if(input != null && input.length > 1) {

            this.inputArr = input;
            this.quickSort(0, inputArr.length - 1);
        }
    }

    private void quickSort(int begin, int end) {

        if(begin < end) {

            int p = this.partition(begin, end);
            this.quickSort(begin, p);
            this.quickSort(p + 1, end);
        }
    }

    private int partition(int begin, int end) {

        System.out.println("Begin partition begin: " + begin + " end: " + end );

        int mid = (begin + end) / 2;
```

```java
        int pivotVal = inputArr[mid];

        while(begin < end) {

            while(inputArr[begin] < pivotVal)
            begin++;

            while(inputArr[end] > pivotVal)
            end--;

            if(begin != end) {
                System.out.println("pivotVal: "+pivotVal+", swap
                 begin: "+begin+" end: "+end);

                //swap the two values
                int temp = inputArr[begin];
                inputArr[begin] = inputArr[end];
                inputArr[end] = temp;
            }
        }
        System.out.println("End partition,
        inputArr:"+Arrays.toString(inputArr)+"\n");

        return begin;
    }

    public static void main(String [] args) {

        int [] arr = {10, 4, 7, 2, 3};

        System.out.println("Original unsorted:  " +
        Arrays.toString(arr) + "\n");

        QuickSort quickSort = new QuickSort();
        quickSort.sort(arr);
        System.out.println("Sorted: " + Arrays.toString(arr));
    }
}
```

Output:

Original unsorted: [10, 4, 7, 2, 3]

Begin partition begin: 0 end: 4
pivotVal: 7, swap begin: 0 end: 4
pivotVal: 7, swap begin: 2 end: 3
End partition, inputArr:[3, 4, 2, 7, 10]

Begin partition begin: 0 end: 3
pivotVal: 4, swap begin: 1 end: 2
End partition, inputArr:[3, 2, 4, 7, 10]

Begin partition begin: 0 end: 2
pivotVal: 2, swap begin: 0 end: 1
End partition, inputArr:[2, 3, 4, 7, 10]

Begin partition begin: 1 end: 2
End partition, inputArr:[2, 3, 4, 7, 10]

Sorted: [2, 3, 4, 7, 10]

In the above partition method for quick sort, the values greater than the pivot are moved to the

a. left
b. right
c. left or right
d. none of the above

Ans: b

Answer Explanation:

In the quick sort algorithm, a pivot element is picked and all the values lesser than the pivot value are moved to the left of the pivot and all values greater are moved to the right of the pivot. This is called partition.

This partition is applied recursively to the subarrays till all the elements are sorted.

In the above sample, the partition operation is applied for begin and end indexes (0, 4) (0, 3) (0, 2) and (1, 2) and the elements are swapped recursively till they are sorted.

Complexity for quick sort is O(n log n). Mostly, quick sort is a better choice than merge sort, but the worst case complexity for quick sort is O(n^2) which is worse than the worst case complexity of merge sort which is O(n log n).

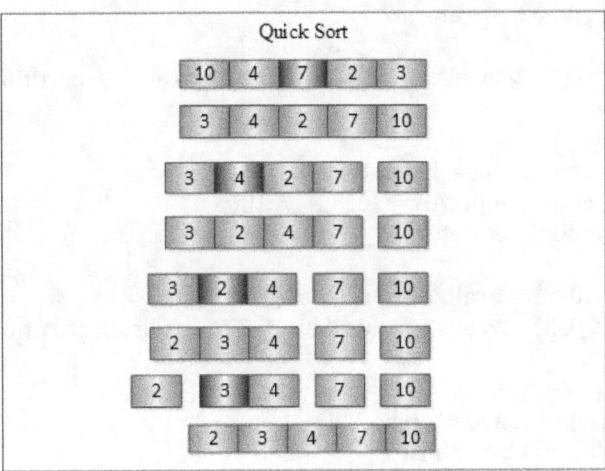

Quick sort performs better when the data is random and also when the data is stored in memory.

Quick sort is an in place sort and doesn't require extra memory for sorting like merge sort. Quick sort is usually a good choice for an efficient and fast sorting algorithm.

Sort functionalities of several language libraries are usually an implementation of quick sort.

inputArr = [10, 4, 7, 2, 3]
quickSort(0, 4) >>>>>

quickSort(0, 4) >>calls>> partition(0, 4)

partition(0, 4) >>
begin=0, end=4, mid=2, pivotVal=7
begin=0, end=4, inputArr = [3, 4, 7, 2, 10]
begin=2, end=3, inputArr = [3, 4, 2, 7, 10]
begin=3, end=3 >>return 3

quickSort(0, 4) >>calls>> quickSort(0, 3) >>calls>> partition(0, 3)

partition(0, 3) >>
begin=0, end=3, mid=1, pivotVal=4
begin=1, end=2, inputArr = [3, 2, 4, 7, 10]
begin=2, end=2 >>return 2

quickSort(0, 3) >>calls>> quickSort(0, 2) >>calls>> partition(0, 2)

partition(0, 2) >>
begin=0, end=2, mid=1, pivotVal=2
begin=0, end=1, inputArr = [2, 3, 4, 7, 10]
begin=0, end=0 >>return 0

quickSort(0, 2) >>calls>> quickSort(0, 0)
quickSort(0, 2) >>calls>> quickSort(1, 2) >>calls>> partition(1, 2)

partition(1, 2) >>
begin=1, end=2, mid=1, pivotVal=3
begin=1, end=1 >>return 1

quickSort(1, 2) >>calls>> quickSort(1, 1) >>calls>> quickSort(2, 2)
quickSort(0, 3) >>calls>> quickSort(3, 3)
quickSort(0, 4) >>calls>> quickSort(4, 4)

2.6.3

```
public class MergeSort {

    private int [] inputArr;
    private int [] tempArr;

    public void sort(int [] input) {

        if(input != null && input.length > 1) {

            this.inputArr = input;
            this.tempArr = new int[inputArr.length];
            this.mergeSort(0, inputArr.length - 1);
        }
    }
```

```java
private void mergeSort(int begin, int end) {

    if(begin < end) {

        System.out.println("mergeSort begin: " + begin + " end:
        " + end );
        int mid = (begin + end) / 2;

        this.mergeSort(begin, mid);
        this.mergeSort(mid + 1, end);
        this.merge(begin, mid, end);
    }
}

private void merge(int begin, int middle, int end) {

    System.out.println("merge begin: " +begin+" end: "+end+"
    middle: "+middle);

    int firstIndex, midIndex, count;
    firstIndex = count = begin;
    midIndex = middle + 1;

    //compare 1st and 2nd half of inputArr and sort in tempArr
    while((firstIndex <= middle) && (midIndex <= end)) {

        if(inputArr[firstIndex] < inputArr[midIndex])

            tempArr[count++] = inputArr[firstIndex++];
        else
            tempArr[count++] = inputArr[midIndex++];
    }

    //copy the rest of inputArr to tempArr
    if(firstIndex <= middle) {

        while(firstIndex <= middle)
        tempArr[count++] = inputArr[firstIndex++];
    }
    else {
        while(midIndex <= end)
        tempArr[count++] = inputArr[midIndex++];
    }
```

```java
        //copy contents of sorted tempArr to inputArr

        for(int i = begin; i <= end; i++)
            inputArr[i] = tempArr[i];

        System.out.println("End merge, inputArr:" +
        Arrays.toString(inputArr) + "\n");
    }

    public static void main(String [] args) {

        int [] arr = {10, 4, 7, 2, 3};

        System.out.println("Original unsorted:  " +
        Arrays.toString(arr) + "\n");

        MergeSort mergeSort = new MergeSort();
        mergeSort.sort(arr);
        System.out.println("Sorted: " + Arrays.toString(arr));
    }
}
```

Output:

Original unsorted: [10, 4, 7, 3, 2]

mergeSort begin: 0 end: 4
mergeSort begin: 0 end: 2

mergeSort begin: 0 end: 1
merge begin: 0 end: 1 middle: 0
End merge, inputArr:[4, 10, 7, 3, 2]

merge begin: 0 end: 2 middle: 1
End merge, inputArr:[4, 7, 10, 3, 2]

mergeSort begin: 3 end: 4
merge begin: 3 end: 4 middle: 3
End merge, inputArr:[4, 7, 10, 2, 3]

merge begin: 0 end: 4 middle: 2
End merge, inputArr:[2, 3, 4, 7, 10]
Sorted: [2, 3, 4, 7, 10]

In the above implementation of merge sort algorithm,

a. mergeSort method divides array to sub arrays and merge method merges two sorted arrays.
b. merge method divides array to sub arrays and mergeSort method merges two sorted arrays.
c. all of the above
d. none of the above

Ans: a

Answer Explanation:

Complexity:

Time Complexity: O(nlog(n)) Space Complexity: O(n)

Explanation:

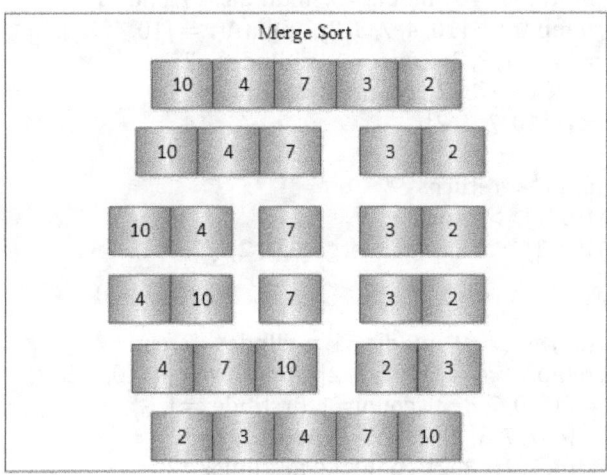

In merge sort, the array is divided into two sub arrays, which are sorted and then merged. The sub arrays are sorted by repeatedly dividing each array into two sub arrays and then merging them again into sorted arrays.

The array with begin and end index (0,4) is divided into two sub arrays with indexes (0, 2) and (3, 4), which are sorted and then merged.

Best case and worst case complexity for merge sort is O(nlog n). Quick sort performs better if the data is random, but merge sort performs irrespective of whether the data is random or not. Merge sort requires extra space while quick sort is an in place sort and doesn't require any extra memory.

Quick sort is faster than merge sort when data is stored in memory. When data is huge and is stored in an external device, merge sort performs better.

arr = [10, 4, 7, 3, 2]

mergeSort(0, 4) >>>>>
mergeSort(0, 4) >>calls>> mergeSort(0, 2) >>calls>> mergeSort(0, 1) >>calls>> merge(0, 0, 1)

merge(0, 0, 1) >>
begin=0, firstIndex=0, middle=0, midIndex=1, end=1
count=0, tempArr = [10, 4, 7, 3, 2] , inputArr = [10, 4, 7, 3, 2]
tempArr = [4, 4, 7, 3, 2], count=1, midIndex=2
tempArr = [4, 10, 7, 3, 2], count=2, firstIndex=1
inputArr = [4, 10, 7, 3, 2]

merge(0, 0, 1) >>returns
mergeSort(0, 1)>>returns
mergeSort(0, 2) >>calls>> merge(0, 1, 2)

merge(0, 1, 2) >>
begin=0, firstIndex=0, middle=1, midIndex=2, end=2
count=0, tempArr = [4, 10, 7, 3, 2] , inputArr = [4, 10, 7, 3, 2]
tempArr = [4, 10, 7, 3, 2], count=1, firstIndex=1
tempArr = [4, 7, 7, 3, 2], count=2, midIndex=3
tempArr = [4, 7, 10, 3, 2], count=3, firstIndex=2
inputArr = [4, 7, 10, 3, 2]

merge(0, 1, 2) >>returns
mergeSort(0, 2)>>returns

mergeSort(0, 4) >>calls>> mergeSort(3, 4) >>calls>> merge(3, 3, 4)

merge(3, 3, 4) >>

begin=3, firstIndex=3, middle=3, midIndex=4, end=4
count=3, tempArr = [4, 7, 10, 3, 2] , inputArr = [4, 7, 10, 3, 2]
tempArr = [4, 7, 10, 2, 2], count=4, midIndex=5
tempArr = [4, 7, 10, 2, 3], count=5, firstIndex=4
inputArr = [4, 7, 10, 2, 3]

merge(3, 3, 4) >>returns
mergeSort(3, 4)>>returns

mergeSort(0, 4) >>calls>> merge(0, 2, 4)

merge(0, 2, 4) >>
begin=0, firstIndex=0, middle=2, midIndex=3, end=4
count=0, tempArr = [4, 7, 10, 2, 3] , inputArr = [4, 7, 10, 2, 3]
tempArr = [2, 7, 10, 2, 3], count=1, midIndex=4
tempArr = [2, 3, 10, 2, 3], count=2, midIndex=5
tempArr = [2, 3, 4, 2, 3], count=3, firstIndex=1
tempArr = [2, 3, 4, 7, 3], count=4, firstIndex=2
tempArr = [2, 3, 4, 7, 10], count=5, firstIndex=3
inputArr = [2, 3, 4, 7, 10]

merge(0, 2, 4) >>returns
mergeSort(0, 4)>>returns

Data Structures

3.1 ARRAY

3.1.1

Given two integer arrays, find if both arrays have the same set of integers.
Eg: For arr1= {1,3,6,10,5,8,2} and arr2= {2,8,5,6,10,3,1} the function should return true.
What is the time complexity for implementing the above functionality using a HashSet?

a. O(1)
b. O(log n)
c. O(n)
d. O(n^2)

Ans: c

Answer Explanation:

Code:

```
public static boolean checkForSameValues(int [] arr1, int [] arr2) {

    HashSet<Integer> set = new HashSet<Integer>();

    for(int i : arr1) {
        set.add(i);
    }
    for(int k : arr2) {

        if(!set.contains(k)) {
            return false;
        }
        else {
            set.remove(k);
        }
```

```
    }
    return true;
}
```

Test Code:

```
public static void main (String [] args) {

    int [] arr1 = {1,3,6,10,5,8,2};

    int [] arr2 = {2,8,5,6,10,3,1};

    System.out.println("Array1: " + Arrays.toString(arr1)+ " and
    Array2: " + Arrays.toString(arr2) + " have same values: " +
    checkForSameValues(arr1, arr2));
}
```

Output:

Array1: [1, 3, 6, 10, 5, 8, 2] and Array2: [2, 8, 5, 6, 10, 3, 1] have same values: true

Complexity:

Time Complexity: O(n) Space Complexity: O(n)

Explanation:

Add contents of array1 into a HashSet. Iterate through the numbers in array2. If the set does not contain the number from array2, return false. If set contains the number, remove the number from the set to avoid duplicates and continue with the iteration.

3.1.2

Merge overlapping intervals

Given (2,5) (3,7) (9,11) merge them to (2,7) (9,11)

For implementing the above functionality, the following static inner class can be used,

```
static class Interval {

    int start;
    int end;

    Interval(int st, int en) {
        start=st;
        end=en;
    }
}
```

If start is greater than the previous end, then don't merge. Otherwise, to merge,

a. replace previous end with current end
b. replace previous start with current start
c. replace previous with current
d. none of the above

Ans: a

Answer Explanation:

Code:

```
public class MergeIntervals {

    static class Interval {

        int start;
        int end;

        Interval(int st, int en) {
            start=st;
            end=en;
        }
    }
```

```java
public static List<Interval> getMergedIntervals(List<Interval>
                                                        input)
{
      if(input==null || input.size() <1) return null;

      List<Interval> output = new ArrayList<Interval>();

      Interval previous = input.get(0);
      output.add(previous);

      for(Interval curr: input) {

            if(curr.start > previous.end) {
                  output.add(curr);

                  previous = curr;
            }
            else {
                  previous.end = Math.max(previous.end, curr.end);
            }
      }
      return output;
   }
}
```

Test Code:

```java
public static void main(String [] args) {

      Interval i1 = new Interval(2, 5);
      Interval i2 = new Interval(3, 7);
      Interval i3 = new Interval(9, 11);

      List<Interval> input = new ArrayList<Interval>();
      input.add(i1);
      input.add(i2);
      input.add(i3);

      List<Interval> output = getMergedIntervals(input);
      for(Interval out: output) {
            System.out.println(out.start + "," + out.end);
      }
}
```

Output:

2,7
9,11

Complexity:

Time Complexity: O(n) Space Complexity: O(n)

Explanation:

Add the first element in the 'input' list to the 'previous' variable.

Iterate through each Interval in the 'input' list.

If the start in the 'current' is greater than the 'previous' end, then don't merge. Otherwise, replace previous end with the larger of the previous or the current end.

Input = (2,5) (3,7) (9,11) >>>>>

previous = (2,5) curr = (2,5) output = (2,5)
previous = (2,5) curr = (3,7) output = (2,7)
previous = (3,7) curr = (9,11) output = (2,7) (9,11)

return (2,7) (9,11)

3.1.3

Given two sorted integer arrays A and B, merge A into B as one sorted array.
You may assume that B has enough space to hold additional elements from A.
The number of elements initialized in A and B are both M.

The above functionality can be implemented by populating

a. first element of B after comparing first elements of A and B
b. last element of B after comparing last elements of A and B
c. using modified binary search
d. none of the above

Ans: b

Answer Explanation:

Code:

```
static void mergeTwoSortedArrays(int []a, int []b, int M ){

        int i = M-1; //last index of a
        int j = M-1; //last index of b with input values
        int k = 2 * M -1; //last index of b with both values

        while(k >= 0) {

                if(j>=0 && b[j] > a[i]) {   //start by comparing last elements
                                           //of b and a
                        b[k--] = b[j--];
                }
                else {
                        b[k--] = a[i--];        //start adding the larger number at
                                                //2M-1 of b

                }
        }
}
```

Test Code:

```
public static void main(String[] args) {

        int _a_cnt = 3;
        int[] _a = new int[100001];
        int[] _b = new int[200002];

        for(int i=0; i< 3; i++) {

            _a[i] = i +1;
            _b[i] = _a[i]+3;
        }
        System.out.print("Before merge A: ");

        for (int i = 0; i < _a_cnt; i++) {
                System.out.print(_a[i] + " ");
        }
```

```
System.out.print("\nBefore merge B: ");

for (int i = 0; i < _a_cnt; i++) {
    System.out.print(_b[i] + " ");
}

mergeTwoSortedArrays(_a, _b, _a_cnt);

System.out.print("\nAfter merge: ");

for (int i = 0; i < 2 * _a_cnt; i++) {
    System.out.print(_b[i] + " ");
}
}
```

Output:

Before merge A: 1 2 3
Before merge B: 4 5 6
After merge: 1 2 3 4 5 6

Complexity:

Time Complexity: O(n) Space Complexity: O(1)

Explanation:

Since size of elements in arrays A and B is M, last index is M-1.

Since B is large enough to hold all elements of A and B together, the last index for all elements in B will be 2M-1.

If last integer in B is greater than last integer of A, b[j] > a[i]), then add this integer to b[k], where k = 2*M-1, which is the last index of B when all elements from both arrays are put together.

If last integer of A is greater than last integer of B, then add this to b[k]. Continue till contents of both the arrays are exhausted.

```
a = [ 1 2 3 ]
b = [ 4 5 6 ]
>>>>>
k = 5, i = 2, j = 2,  b = [ 4 5 6 0 0 0 ]
```

k = 4, i = 2, j = 1, b = [4 5 6 0 0 6]
k = 3, i = 2, j = 0, b = [4 5 6 0 5 6]

k = 2, i = 2, j = -1, b = [4 5 6 4 5 6]
k = 1, i = 1, j = -1, b = [4 5 3 4 5 6]
k = 0, i = 0, j = -1, b = [4 2 3 4 5 6]

b = [1 2 3 4 5 6]

3.1.4

Move all elements of value v to the end of an integer array.

Eg: For array {8,2,4,9,4,7,3,4}, for value v=4 should be rearranged to {8,2,3,9,7,4,4,4}

What is the time complexity for implementing the above functionality?

a. O(1)
b. O(log n)
c. O(n)
d. O(n^2)

Ans: c

Answer Explanation:

Code:

```
public static void moveToEnd(int [] arr, int v) {

    int lastIndex = arr.length-1;

    for(int i=0; i<arr.length; i++) {

        //determine last index that is not v
        while(lastIndex >= 0) && arr[lastIndex] == v) {
            lastIndex--;
        }

        if(lastIndex == 0) { return;} //return if all elements are v
```

```
    if(i<lastIndex && arr[i] == v) {
        //swap v in arr[i] with  last index element
        arr[i] = arr[lastIndex];
        arr[lastIndex] = v;

        lastIndex--;
    }
}
}
```

Test Code:

```
public static void main(String [] args) {

    int [] arr = {8, 2, 4, 9, 4, 7, 3, 4};

    System.out.println("Array: " + Arrays.toString(arr));

    moveToEnd(arr, 4);

    System.out.println("After moveToEnd: " +
    Arrays.toString(arr));
}
```

Output:

Array: [8, 2, 4, 9, 4, 7, 3, 4]

After moveToEnd [8, 2, 3, 9, 7, 4, 4, 4]

Complexity:

Time Complexity: O(n) Space Complexity: O(1)

Explanation:

Iterate through the array. If the integer matches v, swap it with the last element that is not v. If all elements are v, then lastIndex is set to zero and the method returns.

i<lastIndex check ensures that the last swapped elements are not processed again in the iterator.

```
arr = [ 8 2 4 9 4 7 3 4 ] >>>>>
i = 0, j = 7,  arr = [ 8 2 4 9 4 7 3 4 ]
i = 1, j = 7,  arr = [ 8 2 4 9 4 7 3 4 ]
i = 2, j = 6,  arr = [ 8 2 3 9 4 7 4 4 ]
i = 3, j = 6,  arr = [ 8 2 3 9 4 7 4 4 ]
i = 4, j = 5,  arr = [ 8 2 3 9 7 4 4 4 ]

i = 5, j = 5,  arr = [ 8 2 3 9 7 4 4 4 ]
i = 6, j = 5,  arr = [ 8 2 3 9 7 4 4 4 ]
i = 7, j = 5,  arr = [ 8 2 3 9 7 4 4 4 ]
```

3.2 LINKED LIST

3.2.1

```java
public class LinkedListDemo {

    private static class Node {
        int value;
        Node next;

        public Node(int val) {
            value = val;
            next = null;
        }
    }

    public static Node addToLinkedList(Node head, int val) {

        Node n = new Node(val);

        if(head == null) { return n; }

        //iterate to end of list and add
        Node curr = head;

        while(curr.next != null) {
            curr = curr.next;
        }
        curr.next = n;

        return head;
    }

    public static void main(String [] args) {

        Node head = new Node(1);
        head.next = new Node(2);

        addToLinkedList(head, 3);
        addToLinkedList(head, 4);

        printList(head);
```

```
    }
}
```

In the above code, printList prints the linked list values. The final output is

a. 1 2 3 4
b. 4 3 2 1
c. 1 2
d. 3 4

Ans: a

Answer Explanation:

Test Code:

```
public static void printList(Node curr) {

    System.out.println("Print LinkedList: ");

    while(curr != null) {

        System.out.print(curr.value + " ");
        curr = curr.next;
    }
    System.out.println("\n");
}
```

Output:

Print LinkedList:
1 2 3 4

Complexity:

Time Complexity: O(n) Space Complexity: O(1)

Explanation:

To add a node to the LinkedList, create a new node with the integer value. If head is null, then assign the node to the head. Otherwise, iterate through the linked list and add the new node after the last element.

Since the new node is being added at the end of the linked list requiring traversal through all the nodes, the time complexity for add is O(n). If the new node is added as the first element, then the time complexity will be O(1).

3.2.2

```java
public class LinkedListDemo {

    private static class Node {
        int value;
        Node next;

        public Node(int val) {
            value = val;
            next = null;
        }
    }

    public static Node reverse(Node head) {

        if(head == null) return null;

        Node prev = null;
        Node curr = head;

        while(curr.next != null) {

            Node nextItem = curr.next;
            curr.next =prev;
            prev = curr;
            curr = nextItem;
        }

        //point last item to the previous
        curr.next = prev;
        head = curr;
```

```
        return head;
    }

    public static void main(String [] args) {

        Node head = new Node(1);
        head.next = new Node(2);
        head.next.next = new Node(3);
        head.next.next.next = new Node(4);

        head = reverse(head);
        printList(head);
    }
}
```

In the above code, printList prints the linked list values. The final output is

a. 1 2 3 4
b. 4 3 2 1
c. 1 2
d. 3 4

Ans: b

Answer Explanation:

Test Code:

```
public static void printList(Node curr) {

    System.out.println("Print LinkedList: ");

    while(curr != null) {

        System.out.print(curr.value + " ");
        curr = curr.next;
    }
    System.out.println("\n");
}
```

Output:

Print LinkedList:
4 3 2 1

Complexity:

Time Complexity: O(n) Space Complexity: O(1)

Explanation:

To reverse the linked list, two variables 'prev' and 'curr' are used, representing the previous and the current elements.

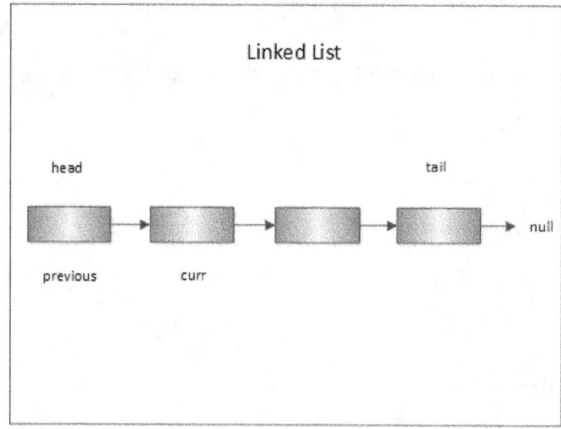

The 'curr' variable is initialized to 'head' and the 'prev' element to null.

For the current node, save the next element to 'nextItem', assign curr.next to the previous node.

Move the previous and current variables to the next elements in the linked list using

prev = curr;
curr = nextItem;

Continue the above iteration till curr.next != null

Finally, after exiting the while loop 'curr' is the last element. Make prev as the next element of curr to reverse it. Also, make 'curr' which is the last element as the head using,

curr.next = prev
head = curr

The time complexity for reversing all nodes in a linked list is O(n).

3.2.3

What is the time complexity for removing an element from a linked list?

a. O(1)
b. O(log n)
c. O(n)
d. O(n^2)

Ans: c

Answer Explanation:

Code:

```
public class LinkedListDemo {

    private static class Node {
        int value;
        Node next;

        public Node(int val) {
            value = val;
            next = null;
        }
    }

    public static Node remove(Node head, int val) {

        if(head == null) return head;

        //if val matches head value remove head
```

```java
        if(val == head.value) {

            return head.next;
        }

        Node curr = head;
        while(curr.next != null) {

            //if val matches curr.next value, remove curr.next
            if(val == curr.next.value) {

                curr.next = curr.next.next;
                return head;
            }
            else {
                curr = curr.next;
            }
        }
        return head;
    }
}
```

Test Code:

```java
public static void main(String [] args) {

    Node head = new Node(1);
    head.next = new Node(2);
    head.next.next = new Node(3);
    head.next.next.next = new Node(4);

    printList(head);
    Node retNode = remove(head, 4);
    System.out.println("After remove: ");
    printList(retNode);
}
```

```java
public static void printList(Node curr) {

    while(curr != null) {

        System.out.print(curr.value + " ");
```

```
        curr = curr.next;
    }
    System.outprintln("\n");
}
```

Output:
1 2 3 4
After remove:
1 2 3

Complexity:

Time Complexity: O(n) Space Complexity: O(1)

Explanation:

To remove an element from the linked list, check if the value passed matches the value in the node. If the head is to be removed, reset the head to the next element.

Iterate through all elements of the linked list. If the element to be removed is the next element to current, then remove the next element by setting

```
curr.next = curr.next.next;
```

3.2.4

What is the time complexity for removing the nth node from end of a linked list?

a. O(1)
b. O(log n)
c. O(n)
d. O(n^2)

Ans: c

Answer Explanation:

Code:

```java
public class LinkedListDemo {

    private static class Node {
        int value;
        Node next;

        public Node(int val) {
            value = val;
            next = null;
        }
    }

    public static Node removeNthNodeFromEnd(Node head, int n)
    {
        if(head == null || n <= 0) {
            return head;
        }

        Node slow = head;
        Node fast = head;

        for(int i=0; i<n; i++) {
            fast = fast.next;
        }

        if(fast == null) {          //if n is list length, remove first node
            return head.next;
        }

        while(fast.next != null) {
            fast = fast.next;
            slow = slow.next;
        }

        //remove the nth element
        slow.next = slow.next.next;

        return head;
    }
}
```

Test Code:

```java
public static void main(String [] args) {

    Node head = new Node(1);
    head.next = new Node(2);
    head.next.next = new Node(3);
    head.next.next.next = new Node(4);

    printList(head);
    Node retNode = removeNthNodeFromEnd(head, 2);
    System.out.println("After removeNthNodeFromEnd: ");
    printList(retNode);
}

public static void printList(Node curr) {

    while(curr != null) {

        System.out.print(curr.value + " ");
        curr = curr.next;
    }
    System.out.println("\n");
}
```

Output:

1 2 3 4
After removeNthNodeFromEnd:
1 2 4

Complexity:

Time Complexity: O(n) Space Complexity: O(1)

Explanation:

To remove nth element from the end of a linked list:

Add two pointers, fast pointer pointing to the nth element and slow pointer to the first element.

Increment both pointers. When the fast pointer is on one before the last element, slow pointer will be on one before the nth from last.

Remove the next element for the slow pointer using

slow.next = slow.next.next

3.2.5

What is the time complexity for removing duplicate elements from a sorted linked list?

a. O(1)
b. O(log n)
c. O(n)
d. O(n^2)

Ans: c

Answer Explanation:

Code:

```java
public class LinkedListDemo {

    private static class Node {
        int value;
        Node next;

        public Node(int val) {
            value = val;
            next = null;
        }
    }

    public static boolean deleteSortedDuplicates(Node head) {

        if(head == null || head.next == null) { return false; }

        Node curr = head;
        while(curr != null && curr.next != null) {

            if(curr.value == curr.next.value) {
```

```
                curr.next = curr.next.next;
            }
            else {
                curr = curr.next;
            }
        }
    return true;
    }
}
```

Test Code:

```
public static void main(String [] args) {

    Node head = new Node(1);
    head.next = new Node(1);
    head.next.next = new Node(2);
    head.next.next.next = new Node(3);
    head.next.next.next.next = new Node(3);

    printList(head);
    deleteSortedDuplicates(head);
    System.out.println("After deleteSortedDuplicates: ");
    printList(head);
}

public static void printList(Node curr) {

    while(curr != null) {

        System.out.print(curr.value + " ");
        curr = curr.next;

    }
    System.out.println("\n");
}
```

Output:
1 1 2 3 3
After deleteSortedDuplicates:
1 2 3

Complexity:

Time Complexity: O(n) Space Complexity: O(1)

Explanation:

Iterate though the linked list. If the current element value and the next element value match, then remove the next element using

```
if(curr.value == curr.next.value) {
    curr.next = curr.next.next;
}
```

Perform the above operation for all the elements of the sorted linked list to remove any duplicate elements.

3.2.6

Duplicates can be removed in an unsorted linked list using:

a. HashSet
b. recursion
c. binary tree
d. binary search

Ans: a

Answer Explanation:

Code:

```
public class LinkedListDemo {

    private static class Node {
        int value;
        Node next;

        public Node(int val) {
            value = val;
            next = null;
        }
    }
```

```java
public static boolean deleteUnsortedDuplicates(Node head) {

    if(head == null || head.next == null) { return false; }

    HashSet<Integer> set = new HashSet<Integer>();
    Node curr = head;

    while(curr!=null  && curr.next!=null) {

        set.add(curr.value);

        if(set.contains(curr.next.value)) {
            curr.next = curr.next.next;
        }
        else {
            curr = curr.next;
        }
    }
    return true;
    }
}
```

Test Code:

```java
public static void main(String [] args) {

    Node head = new Node(1);
    head.next = new Node(2);
    head.next.next = new Node(3);
    head.next.next.next = new Node(1);
    head.next.next.next.next = new Node(2);

    printList(head);
    System.out.println("deleteUnsortedDuplicates: ");
    deleteUnsortedDuplicates(head);
    printList(head);
}
```

```java
public static void printList(Node curr) {

    while(curr != null) {
        System.out.print(curr.value + " ");
        curr = curr.next;
```

```
        }
    System.outprintln("\n");
}
```

Output:

1 2 3 1 2
deleteUnsortedDuplicates:
1 2 3

Complexity:

Time Complexity: O(n) Space Complexity: O(1)

Explanation:

Iterate through the linked list and add the values into a HashSet. If HashSet already contains the next element value, then remove the next element using

```
if(set.contains(curr.next.value)) {
        curr.next = curr.next.next;
}
```

Perform the above operation for all the elements of the unsorted linked list to remove any duplicate elements.

3.2.7

What is the time complexity for finding if a linked list is circular using a fast and a slow pointer?

a. O(1)
b. O(log n)
c. O(n)
d. O(n^2)

Ans: c

Answer Explanation:

Code:

```java
public class LinkedListDemo {

    private static class Node {
        int value;
        Node next;

        public Node(int val) {
            value = val;
            next = null;
        }
    }

    public static boolean isCircularLinkedList(Node head) {

        Node slow = head;
        Node fast = head;

        while(fast != null && fast.next != null) {

            slow = slow.next;
            fast = fast.next.next;

            if(fast == slow) {
                return true;
            }
        }
        return false;
    }
}
```

Test Code:

```java
public static void main(String [] args) {

    Node head = new Node(1);
    head.next = new Node(2);
    head.next.next = new Node(3);
    head.next.next.next = head;

    System.out.println("isCircularLinkedList: " +
    isCircularLinkedList(head));
```

}

Output:

isCircularLinkedList: true

Complexity:

Time Complexity: O(n) Space Complexity: O(1)

Explanation:

Initialize the fast and slow pointers to point to head. Iterate though the linked list and move the slow pointer forward by one node and the fast pointer forward by two nodes using,

```
slow = slow.next;
fast = fast.next.next;
```

If the linked list is circular, the fast and slow pointers will point to the same element after a few iterations. The above function returns true for a circular list and false otherwise.

3.2.8

The most efficient way to get the middle node of a linked list is to traverse the linked list

a. once
b. twice
c. one and a half
d. none of the above

Ans: a

Answer Explanation:

Code:

```
public class LinkedListDemo {
```

```java
private static class Node {

    int value;
    Node next;

    public Node(int val) {
        value = val;
        next = null;
    }
}

public static Node getMiddleNode(Node head) {

    Node slow = head;
    Node fast = head;

    while(fast != null && fast.next != null) {

        slow = slow.next;
        fast = fast.next.next;
    }
    return slow;
}
}
```

Test Code:

```java
public static void main(String [] args) {

    Node head = new Node(1);
    head.next = new Node(2);
    head.next.next = new Node(3);
    head.next.next.next = new Node(4);
    head.next.next.next.next = new Node(5);

    System.out.println("middleNode: " +
    getMiddleNode(head).value);
}
```

Output:

middleNode: 3

Complexity:

Time Complexity: O(n) Space Complexity: O(1)

Explanation:

Initialize the fast and slow pointers to point to the head. Iterate through the linked list and move the slow pointer forward by one node and the fast pointer forward by two nodes using

slow = slow.next;
fast = fast.next.next;

When the fast pointer is pointing to the last element, the slow pointer will be pointing to the middle element.

3.2.9

```
public class LinkedListDemo {

    private static class Node {
        int value;
        Node next;

        public Node(int val) {
            value = val;
            next = null;
        }
    }

    public static void printLinkedList(Node head) {

        if(head == null) return;

        printLinkedList(head.next);
        System.out.print(head.value + " ");
    }

    public static void main(String [] args) {

        Node head = new Node(1);
```

```
        head.next = new Node(2);
        head.next.next = new Node(3);
        head.next.next.next = new Node(4);
        printLinkedList(head);
    }
}
```

The above code, prints

a. 1 2 3 4
b. 4 3 2 1
c. 1 2
d. 3 4

Ans: b

Answer Explanation:

Output:

PrintLinkedList:
4 3 2 1

Complexity:

Time Complexity: O(n) Space Complexity: O(1)

Explanation:

printLinkedList method recursively prints the last element in the list followed by the previous elements.

head = 1 >>>>>
printLinkedList(1)>>calls>>printLinkedList(2)>>calls>>
printLinkedList(3) >>calls>> printLinkedList(4)

printLinkedList(4) prints 4
printLinkedList(3) prints 3
printLinkedList(2) prints 2
printLinkedList(1) prints 1
4 3 2 1

3.2.10

```
public class LinkedListDeepCopy {

    static class Node {
        int value;
        Node next;

        public Node(int val, Node n) {
            value = val;
            next = n;
        }
        Node deepCopy() {
            return new Node(value, next == null ? null :
            next.deepCopy());
        }
    }

    public static void printList(Node curr) {

        System.out.println("Print LinkedList: ");
        while(curr != null) {

            System.out.print(curr.value + " ");
            curr = curr.next;
        }
        System.out.println("\n");
    }

    public static void main(String [] args) {

        Node head = new Node(1, null);
        head.next = new Node(2, null);
        head.next.next = new Node(3, null);
        head.next.next.next = new Node(4, null);

        Node head2 = head.deepCopy();
        printList(head2);
    }
}
```

In the above code, printList prints the linked list values. If executed, the output is

a. 1 2 3 4
b. 4 3 2 1
c. 1 2
d. 3 4

Ans: a

Answer Explanation:

Output:

Print LinkedList:
1 2 3 4

Complexity:

Time Complexity: O(n) Space Complexity: O(1)

Explanation:

In the deepCopy method, each time a new node is created, if next is not null then the deepCopy method is called recursively to create a new next Node.

head.deepCopy() >>>>>

new Node(1) >>calls>> new Node(2) >>calls>> new Node(3) >>calls>> new Node(4, null)

new Node (4, null)
new Node (3, new Node(4, null))
new Node (2, new Node(3, ...))
new Node (1, new Node(2, ...))
1 2 3 4

3.2.11

Time complexity for merging two sorted linked list is O(n) where n is the length of the

a. shorter linked list
b. longer linked list
c. either linked list
d. both linked list

Ans: b

Answer Explanation:

Code:

```java
public class MergeLinkedList {

    private static class Node {
        int value;
        Node next;

        public Node(int val) {
            value = val;
            next = null;
        }
    }

    public static Node mergeSortedLinkedList(Node n1, Node n2) {

        //new node for a merged list
        Node head = new Node(0);
        Node curr = head;

        while(n1 != null || n2 != null) {

            if(n1 != null && n2 != null) {

                if(n1.value < n2.value) {

                    curr.next = n1;
                    n1 = n1.next;
                } else {
                    curr.next = n2;
                    n2 = n2.next;
                }
                curr = curr.next;
            }
```

```java
        else if (n1== null) {

                curr.next = n2;
                n2 = n2.next;
                curr = curr.next;
        }
        else if (n2== null) {

                curr.next = n1;
                n1 = n1.next;
                curr = curr.next;

        }
    }
    return head.next;
    }
}
```

Test Code:

```java
public static void printList(Node curr) {

    while(curr != null) {

        System.out.print(curr.value + " ");
        curr = curr.next;
    }
    System.out.println("\n");
}

public static void main(String [] args) {

    Node n1 = new Node(4);
    n1.next = new Node(7);
    n1.next.next = new Node(9);

    Node n2 = new Node(2);
    n2.next = new Node(6);
    n2.next.next = new Node(8);
    n2.next.next.next = new Node(10);

    System.out.print("n1: ");
    printList(n1);
```

```
    System.out.print("n2: ");
    printList(n2);

    Node mergedList = mergeSortedLinkedList(n1, n2);
    System.out.print("merged list: ");
    printList(mergedList);
}
```

Output:

n1: 4 7 9
n2: 2 6 8 10
merged list: 2 4 6 7 8 9 10

Complexity:

Time Complexity: O(n) Space Complexity: O(1)

Explanation:

Iterate through the two sorted linked lists. If both sorted linked lists have a valid Node, compare the values and add the smaller number to the merged linked list. If only one of the linked list has valid Node, then add it to the sorted linked list and continue the traversal.

While creating the merged linked list, the head can be initialized with zero. Once the elements are added to this list, head.next is returned to skip the first element with zero value.

n1 = [4 7 9]
n2 = [2 6 8 10] >>>>>

n1 = 4, n2 = 2, head = [0]
n1 = 4, n2 = 6, head = [0 2]
n1 = 7, n2 = 6, head = [0 2 4]
n1 = 7, n2 = 8, head = [0 2 4 6]

n1 = 9, n2 = 8, head = [0 2 4 6 7]
n1 = 9, n2 = 10, head = [0 2 4 6 7 8]
n1 = null, n2 = 10, head = [0 2 4 6 7 8 9]
n1 = null, n2 = null, head = [0 2 4 6 7 8 9 10]

return [2 4 6 7 8 9 10]

3.2.12

```java
public class LinkedListCommon {

    private static class Node {
        int value;
        Node next;

        public Node(int val) {
            value = val;
            next = null;
        }
    }

    public static void printCommonElements(Node n1, Node n2) {

        HashSet<Integer> set = new HashSet<Integer>();

        while(n1 != null && n2 != null) {

            if(n1.value == n2.value) {

                set.add(n1.value);

                n1 = n1.next;
                n2 = n2.next;
            }
            else if(n1.value > n2.value) {
                n2 = n2.next;
            }
            else {
                n1 = n1.next;
            }
        }
        System.out.println(set.toString());
    }

    public static void printList(Node curr) {

        while(curr != null) {

            System.out.print(curr.value + " ");
            curr = curr.next;
```

```
        }
        System.out.println("\n");
    }

    public static void main(String [] args) {

        Node n1 = new Node(4);
        n1.next = new Node(5);
        n1.next.next = new Node(6);

        Node n2 = new Node(2);
        n2.next = new Node(3);
        n2.next.next = new Node(4);
        n2.next.next.next = new Node(5);

        System.out.print("n1: ");
        printList(n1);

        System.out.print("n2: ");
        printList(n2);

        printCommonElements(n1, n2);
    }
}
```

Output for the above program is

a. 2 3
b. 3 4
c. 4 5
d. 5 6

Ans: c

Answer Explanation:

Output:

n1: 4 5 6
n2: 2 3 4 5

common elements: [4, 5]

Complexity:

Time Complexity: O(n) Space Complexity: O(1)

Explanation:

To find the common elements in two sorted linked lists, iterate through the two linked lists. If both linked lists have a valid element, compare the values and add to the HashSet if they are equal. Traverse to the next element in both the lists.

If one value is greater than the other, then traverse to the next element of the linked list with the lesser value and continue.

Finally the HashSet will have all the common elements from the two linked lists. HashSet is used to avoid adding duplicate elements.

n1 = [4 5 6]
n2 = [2 3 4 5] >>>>>

n1 = 4, n2 = 2, set = [ ]
n1 = 4, n2 = 3, set = [ ]
n1 = 4, n2 = 4, set = [ ]
n1 = 5, n2 = 5, set = [4]
n1 = 6, n2 = null, set = [4 5]

3.2.13

To find if a linked list is a palindrome, the following can be used

a. binary search
b. reverse
c. recursion
d. HashSet

Ans: b

Answer Explanation:

Code:

```java
public class PalindromicLinkedList {

    private static class Node {
        Object value;
        Node next;

        public Node(Object val) {
            value = val;
            next = null;
        }
    }

    public static Node getReversedLinkedList(Node head) {

        if (head == null) { return null; }

        Node curr = head;
        Node currNode = new Node(curr.value);

        while(curr.next != null) {

            Node nextItem = new Node(curr.next.value);
            nextItem.next = currNode;

            currNode = nextItem;
            curr = curr.next;
        }
        return currNode;
    }

    public static boolean isPalindrome(Node head) {

        Node reversed = getReversedLinkedList(head);

        while(head != null) {

            if (!head.value.equals(reversed.value)) {
                return false;
            }
            head = head.next;
            reversed = reversed.next;
        }
        return true;
```

```
        }
}
```

Test Code:

```
public static void printList(Node curr ) {

        System.out.println("Print LinkedList: ");

        while(curr != null) {

                System.out.print(curr.value.toString() + " ");
                curr = curr.next;
        }
        System.out.println("\n");
}
```

```
public static void main(String [] args) {

        Node head = new Node("K");
        head.next = new Node("A");
        head.next.next = new Node("Y");
        head.next.next.next = new Node("A");
        head.next.next.next.next = new Node("K");

        printList(head);
        System.out.println("isPalindrome: " + isPalindrome(head));
}
```

Output:

Print LinkedList:
K A Y A K
isPalindrome: true

Complexity:

Time Complexity: O(n) Space Complexity: O(n)

Explanation:

To find if a linked list is a palindrome, reverse the linked list and then compare each element in the reversed list with the original linked list. If any of the elements don't match, return false. If all elements match, return true.

3.2.14

Given two linked lists, find the intersection of the two.
Eg: For linkedList1 = 1->2->3->8->10 and linkedList2 = 6->7->8->10 the function should return 8

```
1->2->3->
              8->10
6->7->
```

If both the linked lists can be traversed together such that they meet the intersection element at the same time, then the intersection value can be returned. If difference between the lengths of the two linked lists is n, while iterating through the two linked lists together, start at the nth element of the

a. shorter linked list
b. longer linked list
c. both linked list
d. none of the above

Ans: b

Answer Explanation:

Code:

```
public class IntersectionofTwoLinkedList {

    private static class Node {
        int value;
        Node next;

        public Node(int val) {
            value = val;
            next = null;
        }
    }
```

```java
public static Node getIntersection(Node head1, Node head2) {

    Node n1 = head1;
    Node n2 = head2;

    int len1 =0;
    int len2 =0;

    //find length for the two lists
    while(n1 != null) {
        len1++;
        n1= n1.next;
    }
    while(n2 != null) {
        len2++;
        n2= n2.next;
    }
    //reinitialize to head
    n1=head1;
    n2=head2;

    //increment the longer node to length of diff
    if(len1>len2) {

        int diff = len1-len2;
        for(int i=0; i<diff; i++) {
            n1=n1.next;
        }
    }
    else
    {
        int diff = len2-len1;
        for(int i=0; i<diff; i++) {
            n2=n2.next;
        }
    }
    //increment both nodes till the intersection node is reached
    while(n1!=null && n2!=null) {

        if(n1.value ==n2.value) return n1;

        n1=n1.next;
        n2=n2.next;
```

```
        }
        return null;
    }
}
```

Test Code:

```java
public static void printList(Node curr ) {

    while(curr != null) {
        System.out.print(curr.value + " ");
        curr = curr.next;
    }
    System.out.println("\n");
}

public static void main(String [] args) {

    Node n3 = new Node(8);
    n3.next = new Node(10);

    Node n1 = new Node(1);
    n1.next = new Node(2);
    n1.next.next = new Node(3);
    n1.next.next.next = n3;

    Node n2 = new Node(6);
    n2.next = new Node(7);
    n2.next.next = n3;

    System.out.print("n1: ");
    printList(n1);
    System.out.print("n2: ");
    printList(n2);
    Node intersect = getIntersection(n1, n2);
    System.out.println("Intersect value: " + intersect.value);
}
```

Output:

```
n1: 1 2 3 8 10
n2: 6 7 8 10
Intersect value: 8
```

Complexity:

Time Complexity: O(n) Space Complexity: O(1)

Explanation:

To find the intersection element of two linked lists, find the lengths of both the linked lists. Find the difference in length between the two linked lists. If the difference in length is n, traverse through n elements of the longer linked list.

In the above example, the difference in length between the two linked list is 1, so one element in the first longer linked list is traversed.

Start traversing through both the linked list, starting after the nth element in the longer list and starting at the first element in the shorter list. When the nodes in the two linked list match, return this intersection element.

head1 = [1 2 3 8 10]
head2 = [6 7 8 10]

len1 = 5, len2 = 4, diff = 1 >>>>>

n1 = 2, n2 = 6
n1 = 3, n2 = 7
n1 = 8, n2 = 8
return 8

3.2.15

What is the time complexity for inserting an element into a sorted circular linked list?

a. O(1)
b. O(log n)
c. O(n)
d. O(n^2)

Ans: c

Answer Explanation:

Code:

```java
public class CircularLinkedList {

    private static class Node {
        int value;
        Node next;

        public Node(int val) {
            value = val;
            next = null;
        }
    }

    public static Node insert(Node head, int val) {

        Node n = new Node(val);
        Node curr = head;

        while(curr.next != head) {

            if(val > curr.value && val<curr.next.value) {

                Node temp = curr.next;
                curr.next = n;
                n.next = temp;
                return head;
            }
            curr = curr.next;
        }

        //if val is last element in the list
        if(val > curr.value) {

            curr.next = n;
            n.next = head;
            return head;
        }

        //if val is first element in the list
        if(val < curr.value) {
```

```
            curr.next = n;
            n.next = head;
            //set head as n as it's the smallest value in the list
            head = n;
        }
        return head;
    }
}
```

Test Code:

```java
public static void printCircularList(Node head ) {

    Node curr = head;
    //print all values in the list

    while(curr != null) {
        System.out.print(curr.value + " ");
        curr = curr.next;
        if(curr == head) break;
    }
    System.out.println("\n");
}

public static void main(String [] args) {

    Node head = new Node(2);
    head.next = new Node(4);
    head.next.next = new Node(5);
    head.next.next.next = head;

    printCircularList(head);
    head = insert(head, 3);

    System.out.println("after insert: ");
    printCircularList(head);
}
```

Output:
2 4 5
after insert:
2 3 4 5

Complexity:

Time Complexity: O(n) Space Complexity: O(1)

Explanation:

To insert an element into a sorted circular linked list, traverse the linked list when the next element is not head. If the value to be inserted is greater than the current element value and less than the next value, then insert and return.

At the end of the traversal, current element will be the last element in the circular linked list. If the insert value is greater than this last element, make the insert value as the last element. If the insert value is less than the last element, then insert this value as the first element in the sorted circular linked list.

head = [2 4 5]

val = 3 >>>>>

curr = 2, head = [2 4 5]
head = [2 3 4 5]
return [2 3 4 5]

3.2.16

What is the time complexity for reversing a doubly linked list?

a. O(1)
b. O(log n)
c. O(n)
d. O(n^2)

Ans: c

Answer Explanation:

Code:

```
public class DoublyLinkedListDemo {
```

```java
private static class Node {
    int value;
    Node next;
    Node previous;

    public Node(int val) {
        value = val;
        next = null;
        previous = null;
    }
}

public static Node reverse(Node head) {

    if(head == null) return null;

    Node curr = head;

    while(curr.next != null) {

        Node temp = curr.next;
        curr.next = curr.previous;

        curr.previous = temp;
        curr = temp;
    }
    curr.next = curr.previous;
    curr.previous = null;
    return curr;

    }
}
```

Test Code:

```java
public static void printList(Node curr) {

    while(curr != null) {

        System.out.print(curr.value + " ");
        curr = curr.next;
    }
    System.out.println("\n");
}
```

```java
public static void main(String [] args) {

    Node n1 = new Node(1);
    Node n2 = new Node(2);
    Node n3 = new Node(3);
    Node n4 = new Node(4);

    n1.next = n2;
    n2.previous = n1;
    n2.next = n3;
    n3.previous = n2;
    n3.next = n4;
    n4.previous = n3;

    printList(n1);
    Node r = reverse(n1);
    System.out.println("After reverse");
    printList(r);
}
```

Output:

1 2 3 4
After reverse
4 3 2 1

Complexity:

Time Complexity: O(n) Space Complexity: O(1)

Explanation:

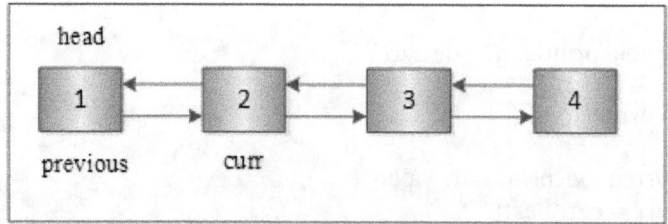

To reverse a doubly linked list, iterate through the linked list and for each element, point next to the previous and the previous to the next. Next move to the next element and continue the reversal.

3.2.17

What is the time complexity for removing a node from a doubly linked list?

a. O(1)
b. O(log n)
c. O(n)
d. O(n^2)

Ans: c

Answer Explanation:

Code:

```
public class DoublyLinkedListDemo {

    private static class Node {
        int value;
        Node next;
        Node previous;

        public Node(int val) {
            value = val;
            next = null;
            previous = null;
        }
    }

    public static Node removeNode(Node head, int val) {

        if(head == null) return head;

        if(head .value == val) {

            head.next.previous = null;
            return head.next;
        }
```

```
        Node curr = head;
        while(curr.next != null) {

            if(curr.next.value == val) {

                curr.next = curr.next.next;
                //curr.next is already curr.next.next
                curr.next.previous = curr;
                break;
            }
            curr=curr.next;
        }
        return head;
    }
}
```

Test Code:

```
public static void printList(Node curr) {

    while(curr != null) {

        System.out.print(curr.value + " ");
        curr = curr.next;
    }
    System.out.println("\n");
}
```

```
public static void main(String [] args) {

    Node n1 = new Node(1);
    Node n2 = new Node(2);
    Node n3 = new Node(3);
    Node n4 = new Node(4);

    n1.next = n2;
    n2.previous = n1;
    n2.next = n3;
    n3.previous = n2;
    n3.next = n4;
    n4.previous = n3;

    printList(n1);
```

```
    Node retNode = removeNode(n1, 3);
    System.out.println("After remove");
    printList(retNode);
}
```

Output:
1 2 3 4
After remove
1 2 4

Complexity:

Time Complexity: O(n) Space Complexity: O(1)

Explanation:

To remove a node from a doubly linked list, traverse through the linked list. If the node to be removed is the head, then make the next node as the head and point the previous to null.

If the value to be removed is in the middle of the linked list, which is curr.next, point to the next element by using

curr.next = curr.next.next;

After setting curr.next to curr.next.next

curr.next.previous = curr;

This will remove the original curr.next element.

3.3 STACK AND QUEUE

3.3.1

```java
public class StackDemo {

    private int [] arr;
    private int nItems = 0;
    private int top = -1;

    public StackDemo(int size) {

        arr = new int[size];
    }

    public boolean isEmpty() {

        return nItems == 0;
    }

    public boolean isFull() {

        return arr.length == nItems;
    }

    public void push(int i) {        //add

        if(!isFull()) {
            arr[++top] = i;
            nItems++;
        }
    }

    public int pop() {               //remove

        int temp = -1;
        if(!isEmpty()) {
            temp = arr[top--];
            nItems--;
        }
        return temp;
    }
```

```java
public void printStack() {

    System.out.println("Print stack: ");

    if(!isEmpty()) {

        for(int i=0; i< nItems; i++) {

            System.out.print(arr[i] + " ");
        }
    } else
    {
        System.out.println("Stack is empty");
    }
}

public static void main(String [] args) {

    StackDemo s = new StackDemo(10);
    s.push(1);
    s.push(2);
    s.push(3);
    s.push(4);

    s.printStack();
    System.out.println("\npop");
    s.pop();
    s.printStack();

    }
}
```

In the above code snippet, what will be the last line of the output?

a. 1 2 3 4
b. 1 2 3
c. 2 3 4
d. none of the above

Ans: b

Answer Explanation:

Output:

Print stack:
1 2 3 4
pop
Print stack:
1 2 3

Complexity:

Time Complexity: O(1) Space Complexity: O(n)

Explanation:

The above StackDemo class represents Stack data structure implemented using an integer array. Insertion and deletion of objects happen according to the (last-in-first-out) LIFO principle.

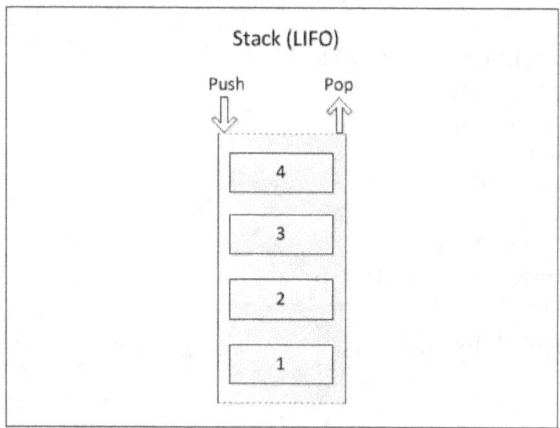

Stack adds to the top and removes from the top which is the last element in the array. Example of a Stack is stacking pancakes one on top of the other as they are being made and then removing the top pancake first.

Accordingly, when 1,2,3,4 are pushed (inserted) sequentially, pop removes the last item that was pushed, which is 4.

Time Complexity for stack insertion (push) and deletion (pop) is O(1).

3.3.2

```
//circular queue
public class QueueDemo {

        private int [] arr;
        private int nItems = 0;
        private int front = 0;
        private int rear = 0;
        private int maxCapacity = 0;

        public QueueDemo(int size) {

                maxCapacity = size;
                arr = new int[maxCapacity];
        }

        public boolean isEmpty() {

                return nItems == 0;
        }

        public boolean isFull() {

                return nItems == maxCapacity;
        }

public void enqueue(int n) {          //add

        if(!isFull()) {

                arr[rear] = n;
                rear = (rear+1) % maxCapacity;
                nItems++;
        }
}

        public int dequeue() {          //remove

        int temp = -1;

        if(!isEmpty()) {
                temp = arr[front];
```

```java
        arr[front] = 0; //remove value by replacing with 0

        front =(front+1)%maxCapacity;
        nItems--;
    }
    return temp;
}

public void printQueue() {

    if(!isEmpty()) {
        System.out.println(Arrays.toString(arr) + "front: " +
        front + " rear: "+ rear);
    } else {
        System.out.println("Queue is empty");
    }
}

public static void main(String [] args) {

    QueueDemo q = new QueueDemo(5);
    q.enqueue(1);
    q.enqueue (2);
    q.enqueue (3);
    q.enqueue (4);
    q.enqueue (5);
    q.printQueue();

    q.dequeue();
    System.out.println("\nAfter dequeue: ");
    q.printQueue();
    q.dequeue();
    System.out.println("\nAfter dequeue: ");
    q.printQueue();

    q.enqueue (6);
    System.out.println("\nAfter enqueue(6): ");
    q.printQueue();
    q.enqueue (7);
    System.out.println("\nAfter enqueue(7): ");
    q.printQueue();
}
}
```

If the program is executed, value 2 in the queue will be replaced by

a. four
b. five
c. six
d. seven

Ans: d

Answer Explanation:

Output:

[1, 2, 3, 4, 5] front: 0 rear: 0

After dequeue:
[0, 2, 3, 4, 5] front: 1 rear: 0
After dequeue:
[0, 0, 3, 4, 5] front: 2 rear: 0

After enqueue(6):
[6, 0, 3, 4, 5] front: 2 rear: 1
After enqueue(7):
[6, 7, 3, 4, 5] front: 2 rear: 2

Complexity:

Time Complexity: O(1) Space Complexity: O(n)

Explanation:

The QueueDemo class represents implementation of a circular queue using an array, where insertion and deletion of objects happen according to the FIFO (first-in-first-out) principle. Queue adds to the rear and removes from the front.

Initially 1,2,3,4,5 are added sequentially, then call to dequeue() twice removes the first two items. 1 and 2 are removed and are replaced with zero. After enqueue 6 followed by enqueue 7, they are added to the first two positions. So, the position occupied by 2 initially is now occupied by 7 and the final output will be 6,7,3,4,5.

Queue is supported in Java as AbstractQueue class which implements the Queue interface. There are multiple classes like LinkedBlocking Queue, ArrayBlockingQueue that extend the AbstractQueue class.

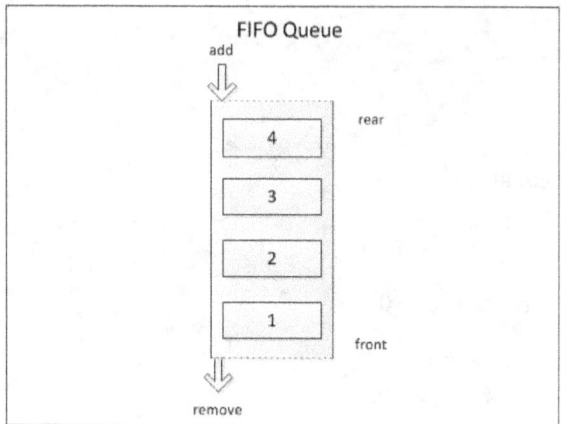

Example is a queue formed in a ticket counter. Person in front of the queue leaves after getting the ticket and a new person joins the queue at the rear. Time Complexity for queue insertion (enqueue) and deletion (dequeue) is O(1).

3.3.3

```
public class StackUsingQueue {

    private Queue<Integer> queue = new LinkedList<Integer>();

    public void push(int a) {

        queue.add(a);
        int size = queue.size();

        //move all numbers to the back of the newly added number
        while(size > 1) {
            queue.add(queue.remove());
            size--;
        }
    }
}
```

```java
public int pop() {

    int val = -1;

    if(!queue.isEmpty())
        val = queue.remove();

    return val;
}

public void printStack() {

    System.out.println("Print stack: ");

    if(!queue.isEmpty()) {

        for(int i : queue) {
            System.out.print(i + " ");
        }
    }
    else {
        System.out.println("Stack is empty");
    }
}

public static void main(String [] args) {

    StackUsingQueue s = new StackUsingQueue();
    s.push(1);
    s.push(2);
    s.push(3);
    s.push(4);
    s.printStack();

    System.out.println("\npop");
    s.pop();
    s.printStack();
}
}
```

In the above code snippet, what will be the last line of the output?

a. 1 2 3 4

b. 1 2 3
c. 2 3 4
d. 3 2 1

Ans: d

Answer Explanation:

Output:

Print stack:
4 3 2 1
pop
Print stack:
3 2 1

Complexity:

Add:
Time Complexity: O(n) Space Complexity: O(n)

Delete:
Time Complexity: O(1) Space Complexity: O(n)

Explanation:

The above StackUsingQueue class represents Stack data structure implemented using a Queue. Insertion and deletion of objects in a stack happen according to the (last-in-first-out) LIFO principle.

Stack adds to the top and removes from the top which is the last element. Queue adds to the rear and removes from the front.

To implement a Stack using Queue, the elements in the front of the Queue are moved to the rear of the new element that is added. The last element added is in the front and can be removed when needed.

When 1,2,3,4 are pushed (inserted) into the Queue, they are reversed. Pop removes the last item that was pushed, which is 4.

Time Complexity for stack insertion (push) using Queue is O(n), as the elements need to be reversed. Complexity for deletion (pop) is O(1).

Stack implementation is done using a Queue which is a LinkedList. Since LinkedList implements the Queue interface, LinkedList object can be assigned to a Queue.

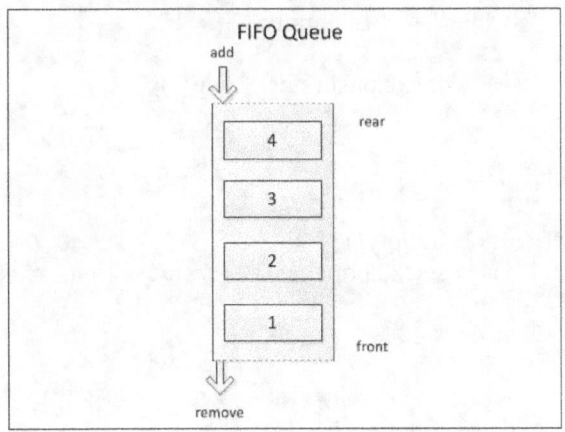

queue = [ ] >>>>>
push(1) >> a = 1, queue = [1], size = 1, queue = [1]
push(2) >> a = 2, queue = [1 2], size = 2, queue = [2 1]

push(3) >> a = 3, queue = [2 1 3], size = 3, queue = [3 2 1]
push(4) >> a = 4, queue = [3 2 1 4], size = 4, queue = [4 3 2 1]
pop() >> queue = [3 2 1]

3.3.4

```
public class QueueUsingStacks {

    private Stack<Integer> stack1 = new Stack<Integer>();

    private Stack<Integer> stack2 = new Stack<Integer>();

    public void enqueue(int n) {

        stack1.push(n);      //add to stack1
    }
```

```java
public int dequeue() {

    //if stack2 is empty push all elements of stack1 to stack2
    if(stack2.isEmpty()) {

        while(!stack1.isEmpty()) {

            stack2.push(stack1.pop());
        }
    }
    int val = -1;

    if(!stack2.isEmpty()) {
        val = stack2.pop();        //remove from stack2
    }
    return val;
}

public void printQueue() {

    if(!stack1.isEmpty() || !stack2.isEmpty()) {

        for(int i : stack1) {
            System.out.print(i + " ");
        }
        ArrayList<Integer> al =
            new ArrayList<Integer>(stack2);

        Collections.reverse(al);

        for(int i : al) {
            System.out.print(i + " ");
        }
    } else
    {
        System.out.println("Queue is empty");
    }
}

public static void main(String [] args) {

    QueueUsingStacks q = new QueueUsingStacks();
    q.enqueue(1);
```

```
        q.enqueue (2);
        q.enqueue (3);
        q.enqueue (4);
        q.enqueue (5);
        q.printQueue();

        q.dequeue();
        System.out.println("\n\nAfter dequeue: ");
        q.printQueue();
        q.dequeue();
        System.out.println("\n\nAfter dequeue: ");
        q.printQueue();

        q.enqueue (6);
        System.out.println("\n\nAfter enqueue(6): ");
        q.printQueue();
        q.enqueue (7);
        System.out.println("\n\nAfter enqueue(7): ");
        q.printQueue();
    }
}
```

In the above code snippet, what will be the last line of the output?

a. 3 4 5 6 7
b. 6 7 3 4 5
c. 6 7 5 4 3
d. 7 6 5 4 3

Ans: b

Answer Explanation:

Output:

1 2 3 4 5
After dequeue:
2 3 4 5
After dequeue:
3 4 5
After enqueue(6):
6 3 4 5
After enqueue(7):

6 7 3 4 5

Complexity:

Add:
Time Complexity: O(1) Space Complexity: O(n)

Delete:
Time Complexity: O(n) Space Complexity: O(n)

Explanation:

The QueueUsingStacks class represents implementation of a circular queue using two stacks.

Stack adds to the top and removes from the top which is the last element. Queue adds to the rear and removes from the front.

Initially 1,2,3,4,5 are added to stack1 after enqueue. When dequeue is called, all elements are popped out of stack1 and pushed to stack2.

Since 1 is the last element added to stack2, it gets popped. During next dequeue, 2 gets popped from stack2. Next two enqueues push 6 and 7 to stack1.

printQueue() method prints the stack1 elements, followed by the stack2 elements in reverse order.

Since all elements are first pushed into stack1 and later popped out of stack1 and pushed to stack2, the element that was added first into stack1 is on the top of stack2. So popping the element out of stack2 removes the first element added to stack1 which replicates the queue functionality.

Time Complexity for Queue insertion (enqueue) using two Stacks is O(1). Complexity for deletion (dequeue) is O(n) as the elements added to stack1 are pushed into stack2 before being popped.

enqueue(1), enqueue(2), enqueue(3), enqueue(4), enqueue(5)
stack1 = [1 2 3 4 5], stack2 = [ ] >>>>>

dequeue() >> stack1 = [ ], stack2 = [5 4 3 2]
dequeue() >> stack1 = [ ], stack2 = [5 4 3]

enqueue(6) >> stack1 = [6], stack2 = [5 4 3]
enqueue(7) >> stack1 = [6 7], stack2 = [5 4 3]

3.3.5

```java
public class QueueReversekElements {

    public static void reverseKElements(Queue<Integer> queue,
                                                        int k)
    {
        if(k > queue.size()) return;

        Stack<Integer> stack = new Stack<Integer>();

        for(int i=0; i<k; i++) {

            stack.push(queue.remove());
        }

        while(!stack.isEmpty()) {

            queue.add(stack.pop());
        }

        //remove the un reversed elements and add them to the back
        for(int i=0; i<queue.size()-k; i++) {

            queue.add(queue.remove());
        }
    }

    public static void main(String [] args) {

        Queue<Integer> queue = new LinkedList<Integer>();
        queue.add(1);
        queue.add(2);
        queue.add(3);
        queue.add(4);
        queue.add(5);

        System.out.println(queue.toString());
```

```
        reverseKElements(queue, 2);
        System.out.println(queue.toString());
    }
}
```

In the above code snippet, what will be the last line of the output?

a. 3 4 5 1 2
b. 2 1 3 4 5
c. 1 2 5 4 3
d. 2 1 5 4 3

Ans: b

Answer Explanation:

Output:

[1, 2, 3, 4, 5]
[2, 1, 3, 4, 5]

Complexity:

Time Complexity: O(n) Space Complexity: O(n)

Explanation:

The reverseKElements() method reverses the first k elements in the queue.

Queue adds to the rear and removes from the front. Stack adds to the top and removes from the top.

In the above method call, k=2 and the queue has five integers [1 2 3 4 5]. The first two elements 1 and 2 are removed from the queue and added to the stack.

Next, 2 and 1 are popped from the stack and added to the queue at the end. Now the first two elements have been reversed and is at the end of the queue as [3 4 5 2 1].

Next, queue.size–k elements which is 3 elements in the queue are removed from the front of the queue and added to the back.

Finally elements in the queue are [2 1 3 4 5] where the first 2 elements have been reversed.

reverseKElements(queue, k)
queue = [1 2 3 4 5], k = 2 >>>>>

queue = [1 2 3 4 5], stack = [ ]
queue = [3 4 5], stack = [1 2]

queue = [3 4 5 2 1], stack = [ ]
queue = [2 1 3 4 5], stack = [ ]

3.3.6

Evaluate the value of an arithmetic expression in Reverse Polish Notation. Valid operators are +,-,*,/. Each operand may be an integer or another expression.

Example: ["2", "1", "+", "3", "*"] -> ((2 + 1) * 3) -> 9

["4", "13", "5", "/", "+"] -> (4 + (13 / 5)) -> 6

Which of the following data structures can be used to implement the above functionality?

a. stack
b. queue
c. linked list
d. binary tree

Ans: a

Answer Explanation:

Code:

```
public class ReversePolishNotation {

    public static int calculate(String [] tokens) {

        String operands = "+-/*";
```

```java
        Stack<String> stack = new Stack<String>();

        for(String val : tokens) {

            if(!operands.contains(val)) {

                stack.push(val);
            }
            else {
                int a = Integer.valueOf(stack.pop());
                int b = Integer.valueOf(stack.pop());

                switch(val) {
                    case "+" :
                        stack.push(String.valueOf(b+a));
                        break;

                    case "-" :
                        stack.push(String.valueOf(b-a));
                        break;

                    case "*" :
                        stack.push(String.valueOf(b*a));
                        break;

                    case "/" :
                        stack.push(String.valueOf(b/a));
                        break;
                }
            }
        }
        return Integer.valueOf(stack.pop());
    }
}
```

Test Code:

```java
public static void main(String [] str) {

    String [] arr = {"2", "1", "+", "3", "*"};
    //String [] arr = {"4", "13", "5", "/", "+"};
    System.out.println(ReversePolishNotation.calculate(arr));
}
```

Output:

9

Complexity:

Time Complexity: O(n) Space Complexity: O(n)

Explanation:

In the calculate() method, iterate through each value in the token. If the value is not an operand, then push into the stack.

If the value is an operand, the two previous numbers are popped from the stack and these numbers are used to compute the result in the case statement. The result is then pushed into the stack again.

This operation is iteratively executed till all the values in the array are exhausted and the final output is computed.

tokens = ["2", "1", "+", "3", "*"], k = 2 >>>>>

val = 2, stack = [2]
val = 1, stack = [2 1]

val = +, a = 1, b = 2, stack = [3]

val = 3, stack = [3 3]
val = *, a = 3, b = 3, stack = [9]

return 9

3.3.7

Given a string that contains any number of letters, numbers or symbols () {} [], the function should return true if the parentheses match up, false if not. For example (a[b{c}d]e) should return true and {goo(db}ye) should return false.

Which of the following data structures can be used to implement the above functionality?

a. stack
b. queue
c. linked list
d. binary tree

Ans: a

Answer Explanation:

Code:

```
public class ValidParentheses {

    public static boolean hasMatch(String inputStr) {

        String tokenStr = "[,{,(,),},]";

        //add the index for all the tokens in inputStr to tokenMap
        TreeMap<Integer, String> tokenMap =
            addTokensFromString(inputStr, tokenStr);

        //if no tokens
        if(tokenMap.size() < 1) {

            return true;
        }

        Iterator<String> tokenIter = tokenMap.values().iterator();

        Stack<String> stack= new Stack<String>();

        //use following map for checking matching braces
        HashMap<String, String> braceMap =
            new HashMap<String, String>();

        map.put("[", "]");
        map.put("{", "}");
        map.put("(", ")");
```

//push the sorted start tokens in the order it appears in the string to the Stack

//when end token is encountered pop the previous one and check if there is a match

```java
while (tokenIter.hasNext()) {

        String token = tokenIter.next();

        if(braceMap.containsKey(token)) {

            stack.push(token);

        } else if(braceMap.containsValue(token)) {

            if (!stack.isEmpty() &&
                braceMap.get(stack.peek()).equals(token)) {

                    stack.pop();
            }
            else {
                    return false;
            }
        }
    }

    if(stack.empty()) {

        return true;
    }
    return false;
}

private static TreeMap<Integer, String>
    addTokensFromString(String input, String tokenStr)
{
    TreeMap<Integer, String> tokenMap =
        new TreeMap<Integer, String>();

    String [] tokens = tokenStr.split(",");
```

//Iterate through tokens

```java
        for(String token : tokens) {

            int index = input.indexOf(token);

            while(index >= 0) {
                //add token and index to the Map
                tokenMap.put(index+1, token);

                index = input.indexOf(token, index+1);
            }
        }
        return tokenMap;
    }
}
```

Test Code:

```java
public static void main(String [] args) {

    String [] str = {"hello", "{goo(db}ye)", "(a[b{c}d]e)",
    "{{(A[]bc[])12}3}"};

    for(int i=0; i<str.length; i++) {

        System.out.println("Token matching for " + str[i] + " is " +
        ValidParentheses.hasMatch(str[i]));
    }
}
```

Output:

Token matching for hello is true
Token matching for {goo(db}ye) is false
Token matching for (a[b{c}d]e) is true
Token matching for {{(A[]bc[])12}3} is true

Complexity:

Time Complexity: O(n) Space Complexity: O(n)

Explanation:

In the hasMatch() method, addTokensFromString() method is called with input string and comma separated list of opening and closing braces. This method returns a TreeMap called tokenMap with the list of braces in the input string sorted by their indices.

Iterating through the tokenMap values gives access to each of the braces in the order that they appear in the input string. The input string needs to be checked if the opening and closing braces are appearing in the correct nested order.

A HashMap map is created with each of the opening brace as key and the corresponding closing brace as value. Each of the iterated tokenMap value is checked, if it's an opening brace then it's pushed into the stack. If it's a closing brace, then the stack.peek() method is called to check if the last value in the stack is the corresponding opening brace.

If there is a match, then the value is popped from the stack. This is continued till all the tokenMap values are exhausted. At the end, if the stack is empty, the method returns true otherwise false.

hasMatch()
InputStr = (a[b{c}d]e) >>>>>
addTokenFromString returns >> tokenMap = 1:(, 3:[, 5:{ , 7:} , 9:] , 11:)

token = (, stack = [( ]
token = [, stack = [(, [ ]
token = {, stack = [(, [, {]
token = }, stack = [(, [ ]
token =], stack = [( ]
token =), stack = [ ]
return true

3.3.8

```
public class ProducerConsumer extends Thread {

    static final int CAPACITY = 5;

    private BlockingQueue<Runnable> queue =
        new LinkedBlockingQueue<Runnable>(CAPACITY);
```

```java
public void accept(Runnable runnable) {
    queue.add(runnable);
}

public void run() { //producer thread

    while (true) {
        try {
            execute(queue.take());
        }
        catch (InterruptedException e) {}
    }
}

private void execute(final Runnable runnable) {

    new Thread(runnable).start(); //consumer thread
}

public static void main(String [] args) {

    ProducerConsumer server = new ProducerConsumer();

    server.accept(new Runnable() {
        public void run() {
            System.out.println("Executing task1");
        }
    });
    server.start();

    server.accept(new Runnable() {
        public void run() {
            System.out.println("Executing task2");
        }
    });
}
}
```

When the above code is executed the output will have

a. task1 followed by task2
b. task2 followed by task1
c. either task1 or task2 first

d. none of the above

Ans: a

Answer Explanation:

Output:

Executing task1
Executing task2

Complexity:

Time Complexity: O(n) Space Complexity: O(n)

Explanation:

In the above sample, the main() method calls server.accept() method twice, for executing task1 and task2. The Runnable object is added to the queue in the server.accept() method. The invoker is the Server object that holds the command in a queue and carries out the request by calling the execute() method .

When the server.start() method is called, the run() method is invoked that calls the execute() method to execute the next Runnable object in the queue. In the execute() method, a new thread object is invoked to run the Runnable task.

In the main method, server.accept() method is called to pass the Runnable task which gets added to the queue, this is the producer that adds the task to the queue.

When server.start() is called, the run() method of the server class is invoked, this is the consumer thread that runs infinitely and takes the Runnable objects out of the queue and calls execute. A new thread is spawned in the execute() method to run each task.

3.4 HASH TABLE

3.4.1

```
public class HashTableDemo {

    private Entry[] buckets;
    int maxSize;

    private static class Entry {
        Object key;
        Object value;
        Entry next;

        Entry(Object k, Object v) {
            key = k;
            value = v;
            next = null;
        }
    }
}
```

In the above code snippet HashTableDemo class represents the following data structure

a. Array
b. ArrayList
c. LinkedList
d. Array of Linked List

Ans: d

Answer Explanation:

The above HashTableDemo class is implemented as an array of linked list. Entry is a static inner class representing a singly LinkedList with key and value along with a link to the next node. Entry array, buckets is an array of linked list.

During insert, if there is no other element in the bucket, then the object is inserted. If there are elements already in the bucket, it's called hash collision. The new object has to be compared with all the objects in the bucket to avoid duplicate key entries.

Since hash table is an array of linked list, the best case scenario is when there is no hash collision and the performance is O(1).

The worst-case scenario is when there is hash collision and all the elements are in the same bucket, then the performance is same as a linked list with complexity as O(n).

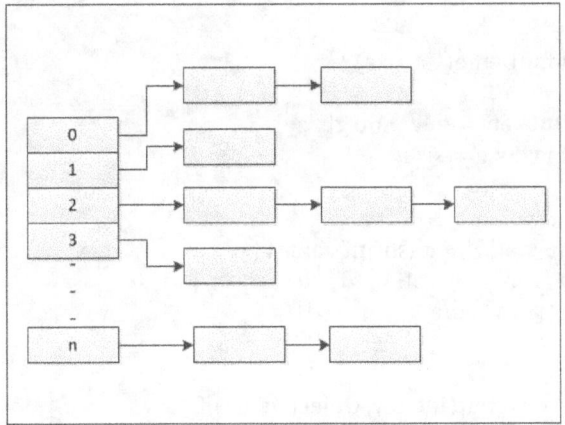

HashTable stores key, value pairs and has very fast add, remove and search of elements with constant complexity.

If there is a hash collision, then the complexity for these three operations will be linear which can be avoided with correct bucket size during initialization. HashTable, HashSet and HashMap classes are supported by Java using hashing for storing data.

3.4.2

```
public class HashMapDemo implements Cloneable {

    Entry [] buckets;
    int maxSize;
```

```java
static class Entry {
    int key;
    Object value;
    Entry next;

    Entry(int k, Object v, Entry n) {
        key = k;
        value = v;
        next = n;
    }
}

HashMapDemo(int size) {

    buckets = new Entry[size];
    maxSize = size;
}

private static int hash(int value) {
    //some operation to calculate hash
    return value;
}

public void put(int key, Object value) {

    //hash(key.hashCode() %maxSize);
    int index = hash(key %maxSize);

    Entry entry = new Entry(key, value, null);

    if(buckets[index] == null) {
        buckets[index] = entry;
    }
    else
    {
        Entry curr = buckets[index];

        while(true) {

            if(curr.key==key) {
                curr.value = value;
                return;
            }
```

```java
            if(curr.next == null) {
                curr.next = entry;
                return;
            }
            curr = curr.next;
        }
    }
}

public Object get(int key) {

    //hash(key.hashCode() %maxSize);
    int index = hash(key %maxSize);

    Entry curr = buckets[index];

    while(curr!= null && curr.key !=key) {

        curr = curr.next;
    }
    if(curr == null) {
        return null;
    }
    else {
        return curr.value;
    }
}

public static void main(String [] args) {

    HashMapDemo hDemo = new HashMapDemo(20);
    hDemo.put(1, 10);
    hDemo.put(2, 20);
    hDemo.put(3, 30);
    hDemo.put(4, 40);

    for(int i=1; i<=4; i++) {

        System.out.println("key: " + i + " value: " +
        hDemo.get(i));
    }
}
}
```

In the above code snippet, with implementation of HashMap get and put, what will be the last line of the output?

a. 1 and 10
b. 3 and 30
c. 4 and 40
d. none of the above

Ans: c

Answer Explanation:

Output:

key: 1 value: 10
key: 2 value: 20
key: 3 value: 30
key: 4 value: 40

Complexity:

Time Complexity: O(1) Space Complexity: O(n)

Explanation:

The hash table is an array of linked lists. Each list is called a bucket.

Hash table is a data structure for finding objects quickly. The hash table computes an integer called hash code for each object using the hashCode() function provided by either the object (eg: String object) or its base class Object.

In the above code, for both put() and get() methods, key is used instead of key.hashCode() for simplicity, with key as an integer. Once hash code is computed, hash code modulo the total number of buckets gives the index of the bucket, where the element should be stored. In the above code hash(key % maxSize) gives the index of the bucket.

If there is no other element in this bucket, then the object is inserted. If there are elements already in this bucket, it's called hash collision. The new object has to be compared with all the objects in the bucket to check if there is a match to avoid duplicate key entries.

If the hash codes are randomly distributed and if the number of buckets are large enough, then few hash comparisons will be needed.

In the put() method, once the index is computed, the new object is added to the corresponding bucket with this index. If this bucket already has one or more elements in the linked list, then there is a hash collision. The object to be added is compared with all the elements. If there is an element already with this key, then the value is updated, otherwise the new entry is added to the end of the linked list.

In the get() method, once index is computed, the element is checked if there is a key match and the value is returned. If there is no key match and there are more elements in the linked list, then all the elements are checked for a match. If there are no elements with the given key value, then null is returned.

```
put() >>>>>
key=1, value = 10, buckets[1] = Entry [1, 10, null ]
key=2, value = 20, buckets[2] = Entry [2, 20, null ]

key=3, value = 30, buckets[3] = Entry [3, 30, null ]
key=4, value = 40, buckets[4] = Entry [4, 40, null ]
```

3.4.3

```java
public class HashMapDemo implements Cloneable {

    Entry [] buckets;
    int maxSize;

    static class Entry {

        int key;
        Object value;
        Entry next;

        Entry(int k, Object v, Entry n) {
            key = k;
            value = v;
            next = n;
        }
```

```
Entry deepCopy() {

        return new Entry(key, value, next == null ? null :
        next.deepCopy());
    }
}

HashMapDemo(int size) {

    buckets = new Entry[size];
    maxSize = size;
}

public Object clone() throws CloneNotSupportedException {

    HashMapDemo result = (HashMapDemo) super.clone();
    //result.buckets = new Entry[buckets.length];

    for(int i=0;i< buckets.length; i++) {

        if(buckets[i] != null) {

                result.buckets[i] = buckets[i].deepCopy();
            }
        }
        return result;
    }
}
```

deepCopy() method in the Entry class copies

a. buckets with and without hash collision
b. buckets without hash collision
c. buckets with hash collision
d. none of the above

Ans: a

Answer Explanation:

Code:

```
public Object get(int key) {

    int index = hash(key %maxSize);

    Entry curr = buckets[index];

    while(curr!= null && curr.key !=key) {
        curr = curr.next;
    }

    if(curr == null) {
        return null;
    } else {
        return curr.value;
    }
}

public void put(int key, Object value) {

    //hash(key.hashCode() %maxSize);
    int index = hash(key %maxSize);

    Entry entry = new Entry(key, value, null);

    if(buckets[index] == null) {
        buckets[index] = entry;
    }
    else {
        Entry curr = buckets[index];

        while(true) {
            if(curr.key==key) {
                curr.value = value;
                return;
            }
            if(curr.next == null) {
                curr.next = entry;
                return;
            }
            curr = curr.next;
        }
    }
}
```

Test Code:

```java
public static void main(String [] args) {

    HashMapDemo hDemo = new HashMapDemo(20);
    hDemo.put(1, 10);
    hDemo.put(2, 20);
    hDemo.put(3, 30);
    hDemo.put(4, 40);

    for(int i=1; i<=4; i++) {
        System.out.println("key: "+ i +" value: "+hDemo.get(i));
    }

    try {
        HashMapDemo hDemo2 = (HashMapDemo) hDemo.clone();

        System.out.println("After clone: ");

        for(int i=1; i<=4; i++) {
            System.out.println("key: "+ i +" value: "+hDemo2.get(i));
        }
    }
    catch(CloneNotSupportedException ce) {
        ce.printStackTrace();
    }
}
```

Output:

```
key: 1 value: 10
key: 2 value: 20
key: 3 value: 30
key: 4 value: 40

After clone:
key: 1 value: 10
key: 2 value: 20
key: 3 value: 30
key: 4 value: 40
```

Complexity:

Time Complexity: O(n) Space Complexity: O(n)

Explanation:

To support cloning, the class needs to implement the Cloneable interface and define the clone() method.

The super.clone() calls the clone method of the base class. Since the base class for the above HashMapDemo class is the Object class, the clone method of the Object class is called.

This clone method of the Object class which provides the default clone functionality, makes a bit-wise copy of the object which is a shallow copy. This works fine if all the fields are of basic type like integer.

If a field has an object reference, then shallow copy will not be enough because the cloned object will also be pointing to the same object reference. In this scenario, default clone functionality will not be sufficient and clone() method should be implemented to make a deep copy.

In the above clone method, for each bucket with a valid entry, a deep copy is made by calling the deepCopy() method of the Entry class. deepCopy() method recursively copies the next Entry element if present. Buckets with more than one Entry element are elements with hash collision.

3.4.4

Populate a HashMap data structure with the name as key and score as value. Next, the program must sort the rows by score and output the top scorers in order of their score. If two students have the same score, then they are sorted by name.

```
public class HashMapSort {

        private static class ValueComparator implements
                                Comparator<String>
        {
            Map<String, Integer> map;
```

```
        ValueComparator(Map<String, Integer> map) {

            this.map = map;
        }

        public int compare(String a, String b) {

            if(map.get(a) > map.get(b)) { //descending order sort

                return -1;
            }
            else if(map.get(a) == map.get(b)) {

                return a.compareTo(b);
            }
            else {
                return 1;
            }
        }
    }

    public static void sortByScore(Map<String, Integer> inputMap) {

        //Comparator and TreeMap to sort values
        ValueComparator vc = new ValueComparator(inputMap);

        Map<String, Integer> sortedMap =
            new TreeMap<String, Integer>(vc);

        sortedMap.putAll(inputMap);

        printTopScores(sortedMap);
    }

    private static void printTopScores(Map<String, Integer>
                                                    sortedMap) {

        for(String key : sortedMap.keySet()) {

            System.out.println( key + " " + sortedMap.get(key));
        }
    }
```

```java
public static void main(String [] args) {

    Map<String, Integer> inputMap =
        new HashMap<String, Integer>();

    inputMap.put("Mike", 57);
    inputMap.put("John", 82);
    inputMap.put("Susan", 99);
    inputMap.put("David", 74);
    inputMap.put("Ann", 98);
    inputMap.put("Kelly", 54);
    inputMap.put("Adam", 98);

    sortByScore(inputMap);
}
}
```

In the above code snippet with implementation of ValueComparator passed to the TreeMap, what will be the second line of the output?

a. Mike 57
b. David 74
c. Ann 98
d. Adam 98

Ans: d

Answer Explanation:

Output:

Susan 99
Adam 98
Ann 98
John 82
David 74
Mike 57
Kelly 54

Complexity:

Time Complexity: O(n log(n)) Space Complexity: O(n)

Explanation:

Comparable interface is used to implement natural ordering of objects. It has one method,

public int compareTo(Object other)

a.compareTo(b) returns zero if a and b are equal, 1 if a is greater than b and -1 if a is lesser than b in the sort order. Objects that implement Comparable interface can be used as keys in a TreeMap or TreeSet.

If the Object added to TreeMap does not implement the Comparable interface, then Comparator interface can be used to define the sort order on the fly. Also if the Object needs to be sorted sometimes by key and sometimes by value, then Comparator interface can be used.

The sortByScore method takes inputMap as an argument. inputMap is populated with name as key and score as value. The rows in the output should be sorted by score. If two scores are same, then ordering should be determined by sorting the names. This is implemented in the ValueComparator.

The compare method takes two keys as parameters. Since score is stored as value in the map, to perform descending order sort, the values are fetched using map.get (key). If the scores are same then a.compareTo(b) is called, a and b are names which are Strings. So compareTo method on the String class is called for sorting the Strings.

In the sortByScore method, a new sortedMap is created and ValueComparator is passed as the argument. Contents of the inputMap are added to the sortedMap. The key value pairs of names and scores sorted by score is printed in the printTopScores method. In the output, Adam and Ann have the same score and have been sorted by name.

Space Complexity for adding an element into TreeMap is O(n), since n elements are added and the time complexity is O(n log(n)).

3.4.5

Populate a HashMap data structure with license plate numbers as key and value. The value of one entry is the key of another entry. The program should print the license plate numbers in sequence with a value followed by another value for which it is the key.

Input:

9THT957, 9EDV008
9EDV008, 7UZO263
7UZO263, 2IBU090
8YLT545, 8PEN016
8PEN016, 9THT957

Output:

8YLT545
8PEN016
9THT957
9EDV008
7UZO263
2IBU090

```java
public class OrderedLicensePlate {

    public static void printSequence(Map<String, String> inputMap) {

        //create a reversed hashMap
        HashMap<String, String> reversedMap =
            new HashMap<String, String>();

        for (String key : inputMap.keySet()){

            reversedMap.put(inputMap.get(key), key);
        }

        LinkedList<String> ouputList = new LinkedList<String>();

        //Get the first key from input Map
        String key = inputMap.keySet().iterator().next();

        String value = inputMap.get(key);

        //Add the first key to the list
        outputList.add(key);
```

```
    //get all the next sequential values from the map
    while(value != null) {
        outputList.add(value);
        value = inputMap.get(value);
    }

    //populate any values before the first value
    key = outputList.getFirst();
    value = reversedMap.get(key);

    //get all the next sequential values from the map
    while(value != null) {
        outputList.addFirst(value);
        value = reversedMap.get(value);
    }
    printLicensePlateNumbers(outputList);
}

private static void printLicensePlateNumbers(List<String> list) {

    for(String str : list) {
        System.out.println(str);
    }
}

public static void main(String [] args) {

    HashMap<String, String> inputMap =
        new HashMap<String, String>();

    inputMap.put("9THT957", "9EDV008");
    inputMap.put("9EDV008", "7UZO263");
    inputMap.put("7UZO263", "2IBU090");
    inputMap.put("4XON750", "8YLT545");
    inputMap.put("8YLT545", "8PEN016");
    inputMap.put("8PEN016", "9THT957");
    printSequence(inputMap);
    }
}
```

In the above code, printSequence method prints the sequence of key value pairs with value being the next key, what will be the first line of the output?

a. 4XON750
b. 9THT957
c. 8YLT545
d. 9EDV008

Ans: a

Answer Explanation:

Output:

4XON750
8YLT545
8PEN016
9THT957
9EDV008
7UZO263
2IBU090

Complexity:

Time Complexity: O(n) Space Complexity: O(n)

Explanation:

The printSequence method has inputMap as the argument which is populated with key value pairs of license numbers. The value of one element is the key of another element and so on which are not ordered.

To print all the key value pairs of the licenses in sequential order starting from the first element of the inputMap, the first key and value are added to the linked list. Then the value is used as the key to search for the next value in a loop. For the last sequential element in the input map, there is no value fetched and the iteration terminates.

There may be more entries in the inputMap for which the first key is the value. To find this, the reverseMap is used, which was created using all the inputMap values as keys and keys as values.

Next, the search is made in the reversedMap. The first element from the linked list is used as the key to search for the value from the reversedMap.

From the reversedMap, rest of the sequence of key value pairs are added as the first element in the linked list iteratively. Finally all key value sequences are printed in order in the printLicensePlateNumbers() method.

3.5 BINARY TREE

3.5.1

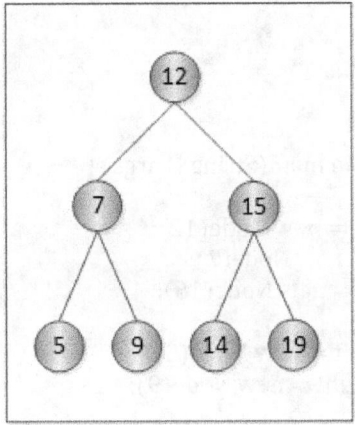

```
public class BinaryTree {

    static class Node {

            int value;
            Node left;
            Node right;

            Node(int val) {
                value = val;
                left = null;
                right = null;
            }
    }

    public static Node lookup(int val, Node root) {

            Node curr = root;
            while(curr != null) {

                    if(val == curr.value) {
                        return curr;
```

```
        } else if(val < curr.value) {
            curr = curr.left;
        }
        else {
            curr = curr.right;
        }
    }
    return null;
}

public static void main(String [] args) {

    Node root = new Node(12);
    root.left = new Node(7);
    root.right = new Node(15);

    root.left.left = new Node(5);
    root.left.right = new Node(9);

    root.right.left = new Node(14);
    root.right.right = new Node(19);

    Node n = lookup(14, root);
    System.out.println("lookup value: " + n.value);
}
}
```

In the above code snippet, a lookup for 14 would traverse through nodes with the following values

a. 12,7
b. 12,15
c. 15,19
d. 7,5

Ans: b

Answer Explanation:

Output:

lookup value: 14

Complexity:

Time Complexity: O(log(n))   Space Complexity: O(1)

Explanation:

In the BinaryTree class above, each node has the data and a reference to the left node and the right node.

The root node is the top most node for the binary tree.

In a binary tree, all values lesser than the current node are saved to the left, and all values that are greater are saved to the right.

In the binary tree above, the value searched is first compared with the root node, if it is less than the root node then its compared with the left node. If the value is greater than the root node then it is compared with the right node. This is continued in all the individual nodes, till a match is found.

For the lookup of number 14, this value is compared with root node 12. Since 14 is greater than 12, it's compared with the right node which is 15. Since 14 is lesser than 15, it's compared with the left node of 15 which is 14 and a match is found.

The above implementation is a balanced binary search tree as the right and left branches on either side of the root node are balanced.

3.5.2

```
public class BinaryTree {

    static class Node {

        int value;
        Node left;
        Node right;

        Node(int val) {
            value = val;
```

```java
            left = null;
            right = null;
        }
    }

    public static void add(int val, Node root) {

        Node n = new Node(val);

        if(root == null) {
            root = n;
            return;
        }

        Node curr = root;

        while(curr != null) {

            if(val == curr.value) {
                return;
            }
            else if(val < curr.value) {

                if(curr.left == null) {
                    curr.left = n;
                    return;
                }
                else {
                    curr = curr.left;
                }
            } else {

                if(curr.right == null) {
                    curr.right = n;
                    return;
                }
                else {
                    curr = curr.right;
                }
            }
        }
    }
```

```
public static void main(String [] args) {

        Node root = new Node(12);
        root.left = new Node(7);
        root.right = new Node(15);

        root.left.left = new Node(5);
        root.left.right = new Node(9);

        root.right.left = new Node(14);
        root.right.right = new Node(19);

        add(21, root);
    }
}
```

In the above code snippet, the new node with value 21 will be added to the right of the following node

a. 5
b. 9
c. 14
d. 19

Ans: d

Answer Explanation:

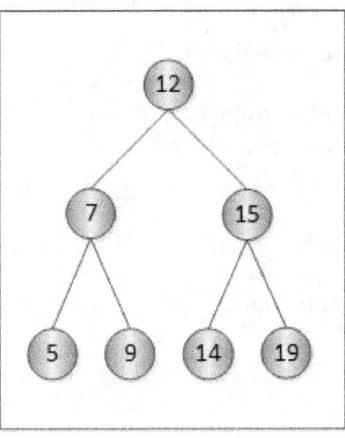

Test Code:

```java
public static Node lookup(int val, Node root) {

    Node curr = root;

    while(curr != null) {

        System.out.println(curr.value + " ");

        if(val == curr.value) {
            return curr;

        } else if(val < curr.value) {
            curr = curr.left;
        }
        else {
            curr = curr.right;
        }
    }
    return null;
}

public static void main(String [] args) {

    Node root = new Node(12);
    root.left = new Node(7);
    root.right = new Node(15);

    root.left.left = new Node(5);
    root.left.right = new Node(9);

    root.right.left = new Node(14);
    root.right.right = new Node(19);

    add(21, root);

    Node n = lookup(21, root);
    System.out.println("lookup value: " + n.value);
}
```

Output:

12
15
19
21
lookup value: 21

Complexity:

Time Complexity: O(log(n)) Space Complexity: O(1)

Explanation:

In a binary tree, all values lesser than the current node are saved to the left, and all values that are greater are saved to the right.

In the binary tree above, the value to be added is first compared with the root node, if it is less than the root node then the left node is checked. If the left node is null, the new node is added, otherwise the comparison is continued with the left node value.

Similarly, if the value is greater than the root node then the right node is checked for null value. If null, the new node is added. If the right node is not null, the comparison is continued with the right node value till the correct position is found to add this new node.

For adding number 21, first it's compared with root node 12, since 21 is greater than 12, its compared with the right node 15. Since again, 21 is greater than 15, its compared with the right node 19. Since 21 is greater than 19 and the right node of 19 is null, 21 is added as the right node of 19.

3.5.3

```
public class BinaryTree {

    static class Node {

        int value;
        Node left;
        Node right;
```

```java
    Node(int val) {
        value = val;
        left = null;
        right = null;
    }
}

public static int height(Node root) {

    if(root==null) return 0;

    return 1 + Math.max(height(root.left), height(root.right));
}

public static void main(String [] args) {

    Node root = new Node(12);
    root.left = new Node(7);
    root.right = new Node(15);

    root.left.left = new Node(5);
    root.left.right = new Node(9);

    root.right.left = new Node(14);
    root.right.right = new Node(19);

    System.out.println("Btree height: " + height(root));
    }
}
```

When executed, the above code snippet prints the following as the Btree height.

a. 1
b. 2
c. 3
d. 4

Ans: c

Answer Explanation:

Output:

Btree height: 3

Complexity:

Time Complexity: O(n) Space Complexity: O(1)

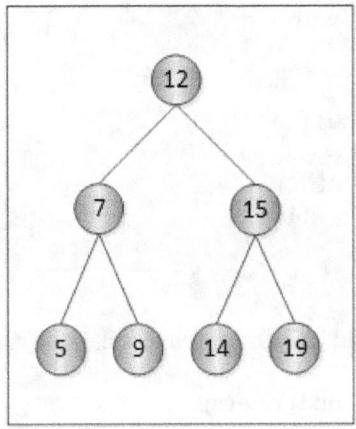

Explanation:

The height method for finding the length of the binary tree returns the height of the current node which is 1 added to height of the left or the right children, whichever is the largest.

root = 12 >>>>>

height(12) >>calls>> height(7) >>calls>> height(5) and height(9)

height(12)>>calls>>height(15)>>calls>>height(14) and height(19)

height(5) and height(9) return 1
height(7) returns 2

height(14) and height(19) return 1
height(15) returns 2
height(12) returns 3

3.5.4

```java
public class BinaryTree {

    static class Node {

        int value;
        Node left;
        Node right;

        Node(int val) {
            value = val;
            left = null;
            right = null;
        }
    }

    public static void levelOrderTraversal(Node root) {

        if(root == null) return;

        Queue<Node> q = new LinkedList<Node>();
        q.add(root);
        int levelNodes = 0;

        while(!q.isEmpty()) {

            levelNodes = q.size();

            while(levelNodes > 0) {

                Node n = (Node) q.remove();
                System.out.print(n.value + " ");

                if(n.left!=null) q.add(n.left);

                if(n.right!=null) q.add(n.right);

                levelNodes--;
            }
            System.out.println(" ");
        }
    }
}
```

```
    public static void main(String [] args) {

            Node root = new Node(12);
            root.left = new Node(7);
            root.right = new Node(15);

            root.left.left = new Node(5);
            root.left.right = new Node(9);

            root.right.left = new Node(14);
            root.right.right = new Node(19);

            System.out.println("levelOrderTraversal: ");
            levelOrderTraversal(root);
    }
}
```

When executed, the above code snippet prints the following as the last line.

a. 5 9 14 19
b. 12 14 15 19
c. 9 15 14 19
d. 14 19 15 12

Ans: a

Answer Explanation:

Output:

levelOrderTraversal:

12
7 15
5 9 14 19

Complexity:

Time Complexity: O(n) Space Complexity: O(1)

Explanation:

Traversal is searching through the tree in a particular order. Level order traversal is also called breath first search. For level order traversal, the root node is first added to the queue.

Then it's removed from the queue and printed followed by adding it's right and left nodes to the queue.

Next, the right and the left node values are printed while adding their children to the queue, which are again printed iteratively. Thus all nodes in each level are added to the queue and are printed in a separate line.

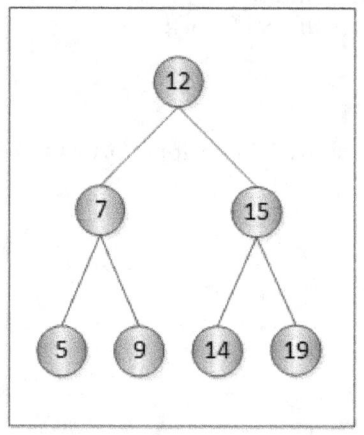

root = 12
q = [12] >>>>>

levelNodes = 1, n = 12, q = [7, 15] >> prints 12 + new line
levelNodes = 2, n = 7, q = [15, 5, 9] >> prints 7
levelNodes = 1, n = 15, q = [5, 9, 14, 19] >> prints 15 + new line
levelNodes = 4, n = 5, q = [9, 14, 19] >> prints 5

levelNodes = 3, n = 9, q = [14, 19] >> prints 9
levelNodes = 2, n = 14, q = [19] >> prints 14
levelNodes = 1, n = 19, q = [ ] >> prints 19 + new line

3.5.5

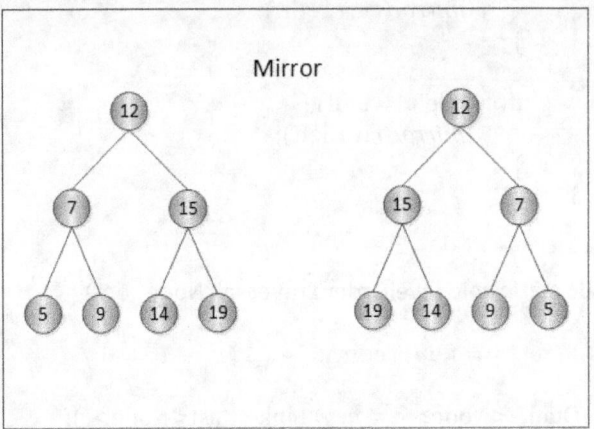

Mirror

```java
public class BinaryTree {

    static class Node {

        int value;
        Node left;
        Node right;

        Node(int val) {
            value = val;
            left = null;
            right = null;
        }
    }

    public static void mirror(Node curr) {

        if(curr == null) { return; }

        if(curr.right != null || curr.left != null) {

            Node temp = curr.right;

            curr.right = curr.left;
            curr.left = temp;
```

```java
        if(curr.right != null) {
            mirror(curr.right);
        }

        if(curr.left != null) {
            mirror(curr.left);
        }
    }
}

public static void levelOrderTraversal(Node root) {

    if(root == null) return;

    Queue<Node> q = new LinkedList<Node>();
    q.add(root);

    int levelNodes = 0;

    while(!q.isEmpty()) {

        levelNodes = q.size();

        while(levelNodes > 0) {

            Node n = (Node) q.remove();

            System.out.print(n.value + " ");
            if(n.left!=null) q.add(n.left);

            if(n.right!=null) q.add(n.right);

            levelNodes--;
        }
        System.out.println(" ");
    }
}

public static void main(String [] args) {

    Node root = new Node(12);
    root.left = new Node(7);
    root.right = new Node(15);
```

```
        root.left.left = new Node(5);
        root.left.right = new Node(9);

        root.right.left = new Node(14);
        root.right.right = new Node(19);

        mirror(root);
        System.out.println("levelOrderTraversal after mirror: ");
        levelOrderTraversal(root);
    }
}
```

When executed, the above code snippet prints the following as the last line.

a. 19 14 9 5
b. 5 9 14 19
c. 9 5 19 14
d. none of the above

Ans: a

Answer Explanation:

Output:

levelOrderTraversal after mirror:
12
15 7
19 14 9 5

Complexity:

Time Complexity: O(n) Space Complexity: O(1)

Explanation:

The mirror method reverses the binary tree. If left or right node is not null then they are swapped. For each of the valid child node, the mirror method is called recursively.

3.5.6

For a binary tree, in order traversal, pre order traversal and post order traversal are also called

a. breath first search
b. depth first search
c. recursive search
d. none of the above

Ans: b

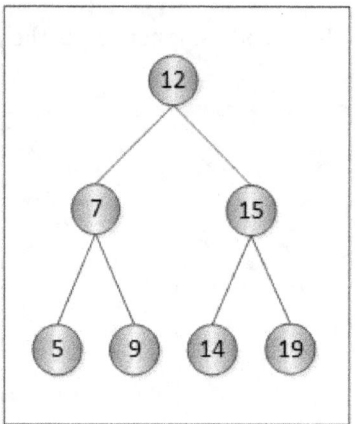

Answer Explanation:

Code:

```
public static void inOrderTraversal(Node node) {

    if(node == null) return;

    inOrderTraversal(node.left);
    System.out.print(node.value + " ");

    inOrderTraversal(node.right);
}
```

```
public static void preOrderTraversal(Node node) {

    if(node == null) return;
```

```
        System.out.print(node.value + " ");

        preOrderTraversal(node.left);
        preOrderTraversal(node.right);
}

public static void postOrderTraversal(Node node) {

        if(node == null) return;

        postOrderTraversal(node.left);
        postOrderTraversal(node.right);

        System.out.print(node.value + " ");
}
```

Test Code:

```
public class BinaryTree {

        static class Node {

                int value;
                Node left;
                Node right;

                Node(int val) {
                        value = val;
                        left = null;
                        right = null;
                }
        }

        public static void main(String [] args) {

                Node root = new Node(12);
                root.left = new Node(7);
                root.right = new Node(15);

                root.left.left = new Node(5);
                root.left.right = new Node(9);

                root.right.left = new Node(14);
```

```
        root.right.right = new Node(19);

        System.out.println("inOrderTraversal: ");
        inOrderTraversal(root);

        System.out.println("\npreOrderTraversal: ");
        preOrderTraversal(root);

        System.out.println("\npostOrderTraversal: ");
        postOrderTraversal(root);
    }
}
```

Output:

inOrderTraversal:
5 7 9 12 14 15 19

preOrderTraversal:
12 7 5 9 15 14 19

postOrderTraversal:
5 9 7 14 19 15 12

Complexity:

Time Complexity: O(n) Space Complexity: O(1)

Explanation:

Traversal is searching through the tree in a particular order. In order traversal, pre order traversal and post order traversal are also called depth first search. These three depth first searches traverse the binary tree differently as shown in the output.

3.5.7

What is the time complexity for converting a binary search tree into a sorted array?

a. O(1)

b. O(log n)
c. O(n)
d. O(n^2)

Ans: c

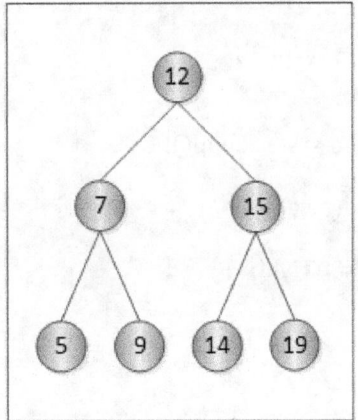

Answer Explanation:

Code:

```
public static void inOrderTraversal(Node node) {

    if(node == null) return;

    inOrderTraversal(node.left);
    System.out.print(node.value + " ");

    inOrderTraversal(node.right);
}
```

```
public static ArrayList<Integer> inOrderTraversalIterative(Node root)
{
    ArrayList<Integer> ls = new ArrayList<Integer>();

    if(root == null) return ls;

    Stack<Node> stack = new Stack<Node>();
```

```java
        Node curr = root;

        while(curr != null || !stack.isEmpty()) {

            if(curr != null) {
                stack.push(curr);

                curr = curr.left;
            }
            else {
                Node n = stack.pop();

                ls.add(n.value);

                curr = n.right;
            }
        }
        return ls;
}
```

Test Code:

```java
public class BinaryTree {

    static class Node {

        int value;
        Node left;
        Node right;

        Node(int val) {
            value = val;
            left = null;
            right = null;
        }
    }

    public static void main(String [] args) {

        Node root = new Node(12);
        root.left = new Node(7);
        root.right = new Node(15);
```

```
        root.left.left = new Node(5);
        root.left.right = new Node(9);

        root.right.left = new Node(14);
        root.right.right = new Node(19);

        System.out.println("inOrderTraversal: ");
        inOrderTraversal(root);

        ArrayList<Integer> inOrderList
            = inOrderTraversalIterative(root);

        System.out.println("\n\ninOrderTraversalIterative: " +
        inOrderList.toString());
    }
}
```

Output:

inOrderTraversal: 5 7 9 12 14 15 19
inOrderTraversalIterative: [5, 7, 9, 12, 14, 15, 19]

Complexity:

Time Complexity: O(n) Space Complexity: O(n)

Explanation:

Traversal is searching through the tree in a particular order. In order traversal is also called depth first search.

For in order traversal, the root node is first pushed to a stack. All the left children are pushed to the stack one after the other and then popped and added to the array. If there are any right child for the value that is popped, the right child is pushed to the stack next and then popped and added to the array.

Since all the values in the left sub trees are less than the root and all values of the right sub trees are greater than the root, all node values are added in ascending sorted order into the output array with this algorithm.

root = 12

curr = 12 >>>>>
stack = [12], curr = 7, ls = [ ]
stack = [7, 12], curr = 5, ls = [ ]
stack = [5, 7, 12], curr = null, ls = [ ]
stack = [7, 12], curr = null, ls = [5]
stack = [12], curr = 9, ls = [5, 7]

stack = [9, 12], curr = null, ls = [5, 7]
stack = [12], curr = null, ls = [5, 7, 9]
stack = [ ], curr = 15, ls = [5, 7, 9, 12]
stack = [15], curr = 14, ls = [5, 7, 9, 12]
stack = [14, 15], curr = null, ls = [5, 7, 9, 12]
stack = [15], curr = null, ls = [5, 7, 9, 12, 14]

stack = [ ], curr = 19, ls = [5, 7, 9, 12, 14, 15]
stack = [19], curr = null, ls = [5, 7, 9, 12, 14, 15]
stack = [ ], curr = null, ls = [5, 7, 9, 12, 14, 15, 19]

3.5.8

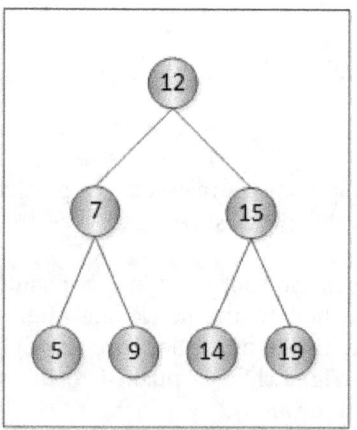

public static boolean isValidBST(Node root) {

    return isValidBST(root, Double.*NEGATIVE_INFINITY*,
                Double.*POSITIVE_INFINITY*);

}

```java
public static boolean isValidBST(Node node, double min, double max) {

    if(node == null) return true;

    if(node.value <= min || node.value >= max) return false;

    return isValidBST(node.left, min, node.value) &&
        isValidBST(node.right, node.value, max);
}
```

What is the time complexity for the above isValidBST method?

a. O(1)
b. O(log n)
c. O(n)
d. O(n^2)

Ans: c

Answer Explanation:

Test Code:

```java
public class BinaryTree {

    static class Node {

        int value;
        Node left;
        Node right;

        Node(int val) {
            value = val;
            left = null;
            right = null;
        }
    }

    public static void main(String [] args) {

        Node root = new Node(12);
        root.left = new Node(7);
        root.right = new Node(15);
```

```
        root.left.left = new Node(5);
        root.left.right = new Node(9);

        root.right.left = new Node(14);
        root.right.right = new Node(19);

        System.out.println("isValidBST: " + isValidBST(root));
    }
}
```

Output:

isValidBST: true

Complexity:

Time Complexity: O(n) Space Complexity: O(1)

Explanation:

isValidBST method is called iteratively to check if value of each left node is lesser than the parent node or the value of each right node is greater than the parent node. If not, false is returned otherwise true is returned at the end of the iteration.

root = 12 >>>>>
isValidBST(12, NEG_INF, POS_INF) >>calls>> isValidBST(7, NEG_INF, 12) and isValidBST(15, 12, POS_INF)

isValidBST(7, NEG_INF, 12) >>calls>> isValidBST(5, NEG_INF, 7) and isValidBST(9, 7, POS_INF)

isValidBST(15, 12, POS_INF) >>calls>> isValidBST(14, NEG_INF, 15) and isValidBST(19, 15, POS_INF)

all the above methods return true to the caller

isValidBST(12, NEG_INF, POS_INF) returns true

3.5.9

```java
public class BinaryTree {

    static class Node {

        int value;
        Node left;
        Node right;

        Node(int val) {
            value = val;
            left = null;
            right = null;
        }
    }

    static int index1=0;
    public static void kthSmallestRecursive(Node node, int k) {

        if(node == null) return;

        kthSmallestRecursive(node.left, k);

        if(++index1 == k) {
            System.out.print(node.value);
            return;
        }
        kthSmallestRecursive(node.right, k);
    }

    static int index2=0;
    public static void kthLargestRecursive(Node node, int k) {

        if(node == null) return;

        kthLargestRecursive(node.right, k);

        if(++index2 == k) {
            System.out.print(node.value);
            return;
        }
        kthLargestRecursive(node.left, k);
```

```
        }

    public static void main(String [] args) {

            Node root = new Node(12);
            root.left = new Node(7);
            root.right = new Node(15);

            root.left.left = new Node(5);
            root.left.right = new Node(9);

            root.right.left = new Node(14);
            root.right.right = new Node(19);

            int k = 3;
            System.out.print("3rd smallest element is: ");
            kthSmallestRecursive(root, k);

            System.out.print("\n3rd largest element is: ");
            kthLargestRecursive(root, k);
        }
}
```

The above code snippet, when executed returns the following values for the 3rd smallest and largest elements

a. 9 and 15
b. 7 and 15
c. 7 and 14
d. 9 and 14

Ans: d

Answer Explanation:

Output:

3rd smallest element is: 9
3rd largest element is: 14

Complexity:

Time Complexity: O(n) Space Complexity: O(1)

Explanation:

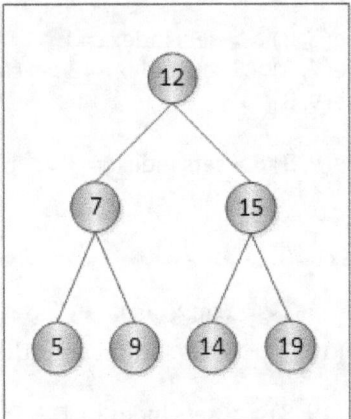

The kthSmallestRecursive and kthLargestRecursive methods use in order traversal for finding the kth element. Traversal is searching through the tree in a particular order. In order traversal is also called depth first search.

In order traversal can be used for sorting the binary search tree in ascending or descending order. The kth element during ascending or descending traversal can be returned to find the kth smallest or largest element.

Since all the elements in the left sub tree of the root have values less than the root, the kthSmallestRecursive method calls recursively all the left nodes and then any of their right nodes.

The index is incremented for each value in ascending order and when the index matches k then the value is printed which is the kth smallest element. Similarly, the kthLargestRecursive method calls recursively all the right nodes and then any of their left nodes and prints them.

The index is incremented for each value in descending order and when the index matches k, the value is printed to access the kth largest element. This works as all the elements in the right sub tree of the root have values greater than the root.

kthSmallestRecursive node = 12, k=3, index1=0 >>>>>

kthSmallestRecursive(12, 3) >>calls>>
kthSmallestRecursive(7, 3)>>calls>>kthSmallestRecursive(5, 3)

kthSmallestRecursive(5, 3) >> sets index1=1
kthSmallestRecursive(7, 3)>> sets index1=2 >>calls>>
kthSmallestRecursive(9, 3)

kthSmallestRecursive(9, 3)>> sets index1=3 >> prints 9

kthLargestRecursive
node = 12, k=3, index1=0 >>>>>

thLargestRecursive(12, 3) >>calls>>
kthLargestRecursive(15, 3)>>calls>>kthLargestRecursive(19, 3)

kthLargestRecursive(19, 3) >> sets index1=1
kthLargestRecursive(15, 3)>> sets index1=2 >>calls>>
kthLargestRecursive(14, 3)

kthLargestRecursive(14, 3)>> sets index1=3 >> prints 14

3.5.10

```java
public class BinaryTree {

    static class Node {

        int value;
        Node left;
        Node right;

        Node(int val) {
            value = val;
            left = null;
            right = null;
        }
    }

    public static int kthSmallestElement(Node root, int k) {

        //inOrder traversal
```

```java
        Stack<Node> stack = new Stack<Node>();
        Node curr = root;

        while(curr != null || !stack.isEmpty()) {

            if(curr != null) {
                stack.push(curr);

                curr = curr.left;
            } else {
                Node n = stack.pop();

                if(--k == 0) { return n.value; }

                curr = n.right;
            }
        }
        return 0;
    }

    public static int kthLargestElement(Node root, int k) {

        //inOrder traversal
        Stack<Node> stack = new Stack<Node>();
        Node curr = root;

        while(curr != null || !stack.isEmpty()) {

            if(curr != null) {
                stack.push(curr);

                curr = curr.right;
            } else {
                Node n = stack.pop();

                if(--k == 0) { return n.value; }

                curr = n.left;
            }
        }
        return 0;
    }
```

```java
public static void main(String [] args) {

    Node root = new Node(12);
    root.left = new Node(7);
    root.right = new Node(15);

    root.left.left = new Node(5);
    root.left.right = new Node(9);

    root.right.left = new Node(14);
    root.right.right = new Node(19);

    System.out.println("3rd smallest element is: "
    +kthSmallestElement(root, 3));

    System.out.println("3rd largest element is: "
    +kthLargestElement(root, 3));
    }
}
```

The above code snippet, when executed returns the following values for the 3rd smallest and largest elements

a. 9 and 15
b. 9 and 14
c. 7 and 14
d. 7 and 15

Ans: b

Answer Explanation:

Output:

3rd smallest element is: 9
3rd largest element is: 14

Complexity:

Time Complexity: O(n) Space Complexity: O(1)

Explanation:

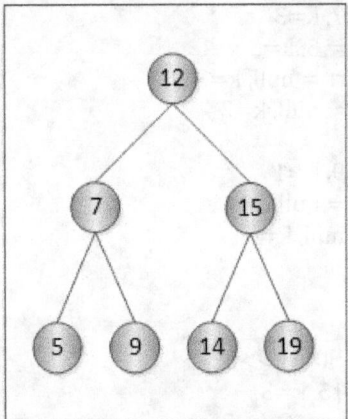

The kthSmallestElement and kthLargestElement methods use in order traversal for finding the kth element. Traversal is searching through the tree in a particular order. In order traversal is also called depth first search.

In order traversal can be used for sorting the binary search tree in ascending or descending order. The kth element during ascending or descending traversal can be returned to find the kth smallest or largest element.

For in order traversal in the kthSmallestElement method, the root node is first pushed to a stack. All the left children are pushed to the stack one after the other and then popped. If there are any right child for the value that is popped, the right child is pushed to the stack next and then popped.

Since all the values in the left sub trees are less than the root and all values of the right sub trees are greater than the root, all node values are accessed in ascending sorted order and the kth element is returned.

For in order traversal in the kthLargestElement method, all right children are pushed to the stack and popped. For the value that is popped, the left child is pushed to the stack and then popped.

The node values are accessed in descending order of which the kth element is returned.

kthSmallestElement
root = 12, curr = 12, k=3 >>>>>
stack = [12], curr = 7, k=3
stack = [7, 12], curr = 5, k=3
stack = [5, 7, 12], curr = null, k=3
stack = [7, 12], curr = null, k=2

stack = [12], curr = 9, k=1
stack = [9, 12], curr = null, k=1
stack = [12], curr = null, k=0
returns 9

kthLargestElement
root = 12, curr = 12, k=3 >>>>>
stack = [12], curr = 15, k=3
stack = [15, 12], curr = 19, k=3
stack = [19, 15, 12], curr = null, k=3
stack = [15, 12], curr = null, k=2

stack = [12], curr = 14, k=1
stack = [14, 12], curr = null, k=1
stack = [12], curr = null, k=0
returns 14

3.5.11

```java
public class BinaryTree {

    static class Node {

        int value;
        Node left;
        Node right;

        Node(int val) {
            value = val;
            left = null;
            right = null;
        }
    }
```

```java
public static int minElement(Node root) {

    if(root == null) return -1;

    Node curr = root;

    while(curr.left != null) curr = curr.left;

    return curr.value;
}

public static int maxElement(Node root) {

    if(root == null) return -1;

    Node curr = root;

    while(curr.right != null) curr = curr.right;

    return curr.value;
}
public static void main(String [] args) {

    Node root = new Node(12);

    root.left = new Node(7);
    root.right = new Node(15);

    root.left.left = new Node(5);
    root.left.right = new Node(9);

    root.right.left = new Node(14);
    root.right.right = new Node(19);

    System.out.println("min element is: " + minElement(root));

    System.out.println("max element is: " + maxElement(root));
}
}
```

The above code snippet returns the following values as min and max elements

a. 5 and 19
b. 9 and 14
c. 7 and 15
d. 7 and 19

Ans: a

Answer Explanation:

Output:

min element is: 5
max element is: 19

Complexity:

Time Complexity: O(log(n)) Space Complexity: O(1)

Explanation:

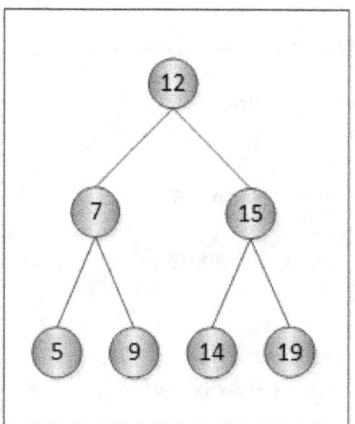

In a Binary search tree all values in the left sub trees are less than the root and the left child value is less than the node value.

In the minElement() method, the left most node in the left subtree of the binary tree is accessed using iteration and it's value is returned.

Since the right child in each node has value greater than the node value, the right most node value is accessed iteratively and returned by the maxElement() method.

3.5.12

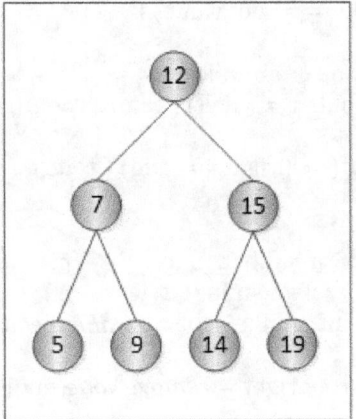

```
public class BinaryTree {

    static class Node {

        int value;
        Node left;
        Node right;

        Node(int val) {
            value = val;
            left = null;
            right = null;
        }
    }

    public static Node removeNode(int value, Node root) {

        if (root == null) return null;
```

```java
    if(value < root.value) {

        root.left = removeNode(value, root.left);
    }
    else if(value > root.value) {

        root.right = removeNode(value, root.right);
    }
    else if(value == root.value) {

        //if one or no child
        if(root.left == null) { return root.right; }

        else if(root.right == null) { return root.left; }

        else {
            //if both children are present, remove smallest
            //element in the right subtree and make it the root
            int minElement = minElement(root.right);

            root.right = removeNode(minElement, root.right);

            root.value = minElement;
        }
    }
    return root;
}

public static void levelOrderTraversal(Node root) {

    if(root == null) return;

    Queue<Node> q = new LinkedList<Node>();
    q.add(root);
    int levelNodes = 0;

    while(!q.isEmpty()) {

        levelNodes = q.size();

        while(levelNodes > 0) {

            Node n = (Node) q.remove();
```

```
        System.out.print(n.value + " ");

        if(n.left!=null) q.add(n.left);

        if(n.right!=null) q.add(n.right);

        levelNodes--;
    }
    System.out.println(" ");
    }
}

public static void main(String [] args) {

    Node root = new Node(12);
    root.left = new Node(7);
    root.right = new Node(15);

    root.left.left = new Node(5);
    root.left.right = new Node(9);

    root.right.left = new Node(14);
    root.right.right = new Node(19);

    System.out.println("levelOrderTraversal: ");
    levelOrderTraversal(root);

    removeNode(12, root);
    System.out.println("\nAfter removeNode,
    levelOrderTraversal: ");
    levelOrderTraversal(root);
    }
}
```

The last line of the output after executing the above code is

a. 5 9 14 19
b. 5 9 19
c. 9 14 19
d. 5 9 14

Ans: b

Answer Explanation:

Output:

levelOrderTraversal:
12
7 15
5 9 14 19

After removeNode, levelOrderTraversal:
14
7 15
5 9 19

Complexity:

Time Complexity: $O(\log(n))$ Space Complexity: $O(1)$

Explanation:

In the removeNode method, if the value to be removed is less than the root value then the left node is replaced by return value of the removeNode method called recursively by passing the left node value.

Similarly if value to be removed is greater than root value then the right node is replaced by return value of the removeNode method called recursively by passing the right node value.

If the value to be removed matches the node value and if one of the children is null, the other child is returned.

If the value to be removed matches the node value, and if both children are present, then the smallest value in the right subtree is fetched using the minElement method and this value replaces the root node value.

removeNode(int val, Node root) >>>>>
root =12, root.right=15, minElement(15)=14

removeNode(12, 12) >>calls>> root.right = removeNode(14, 15)

root=15
removeNode(14, 15) >>calls>> root.left = removeNode(14, 14)

removeNode(14, 14) returns null

root=15
removeNode(14, 15)>> sets root.left=null returns root.value=15

root=12
removeNode(12, 12)>> sets root.right=15>> sets root.value =14

3.5.13

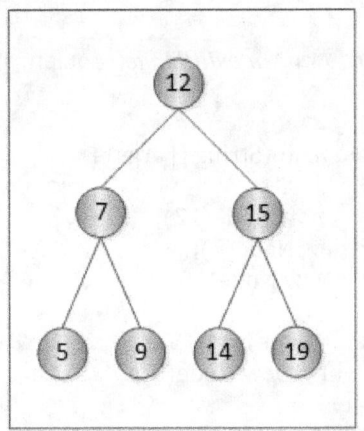

public class BinaryTree {

    static class Node {

        int value;
        Node left;
        Node right;

        Node(int val) {
            value = val;
            left = null;
            right = null;
        }
    }

```java
public static int findNodesInRange(Node root, int min, int max) {

    if(root == null) return 0;

    if(root.value >= min && root.value <= max) {

        return 1 + findNodesInRange(root.left, min, max) +
        findNodesInRange(root.right, min, max);
    }
    else if(root.value < min) {

        return findNodesInRange(root.right, min, max);
    }
    else {
        return findNodesInRange(root.left, min, max);
    }
}
public static void main(String [] args) {

    Node root = new Node(12);
    root.left = new Node(7);
    root.right = new Node(15);

    root.left.left = new Node(5);
    root.left.right = new Node(9);

    root.right.left = new Node(14);
    root.right.right = new Node(19);

    System.out.println("Num nodes in range 12 to 20 is: " +
    findNodesInRange(root, 12, 20));
    }
}
```

The above code on execution will return
a. 2
b. 3
c. 4
d. 5

Ans: c

Answer Explanation:

Output:

Number of nodes in range 12 to 20 is: 4

Complexity:

Time Complexity: O(n) Space Complexity: O(1)

Explanation:

The findNodesInRange method returns the number of nodes in the binary search tree that have the value between the range of min and max values passed.

If the node value falls within the range of min and max, the method returns 1 in addition to the return values of the right and left nodes called recursively with the min and max values.

If the node value is less than the minimum value, then the right node is passed to the recursive function, otherwise the left node is passed.

findNodesInRange(root, min, max) >>>>>

findNodesInRange(12, 12, 20) >>calls>> findNodesInRange(7, 12, 20) and findNodesInRange(15, 12, 20)

findNodesInRange(7, 12, 20) >>calls>> findNodesInRange(9, 12, 20)

findNodesInRange(15, 12, 20) >>calls>> findNodesInRange(14, 12, 20) and findNodesInRange(19, 12, 20)

findNodesInRange(14, 12, 20) and findNodesInRange(19, 12, 20) both return 1

findNodesInRange(15, 12, 20) returns 3

findNodesInRange(9, 12, 20) returns 0

findNodesInRange(7, 12, 20) returns 0

findNodesInRange(12, 12, 20) returns 4

3.5.14

To implement a method that returns an arrayList with values [2, 1, +, 3, *] in the reverse polish notation for the above binary tree, the following traversal can be used.

a. level order traversal
b. in order traversal
c. pre order traversal
d. post order traversal

Ans: d

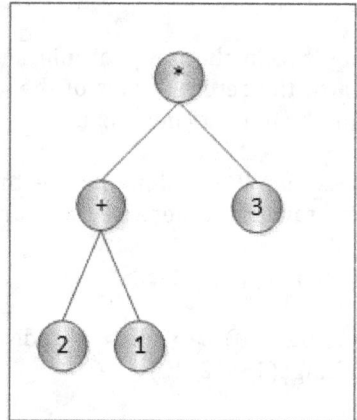

Answer Explanation:

Code:

```
public class BinaryTreeCompute {

        private static class Node {

                String value;
                Node left;
                Node right;

                Node(String val) {
                        value = val;
                        left = null;
```

```java
                right = null;
            }
        }

    public static ArrayList<String>
        postOrderTraversalIterative(Node root)
    {

        ArrayList<String> al = new ArrayList<String>();

        Stack<Node> s1 = new Stack<Node>();
        Stack<Node> s2 = new Stack<Node>();

        s1.push(root);

        while(!s1.isEmpty()) {

            //remove the Node from stack1 and push it to stack2
            Node curr = s1.pop();
            s2.push(curr);

            //push the left and the right nodes to stack1
            if(curr.left != null) s1.push(curr.left);

            if(curr.right != null) s1.push(curr.right);
        }

        while(!s2.isEmpty()) {

            al.add(s2.pop().value);
        }
        return al;
        }
    }
```

Test Code:

```java
public static void main(String [] args) {

    Node root = new Node("*");

    root.left = new Node("+");
    root.right = new Node("3");
```

```
    root.left.left = new Node("2");
    root.left.right = new Node("1");

    ArrayList<String> al =
        postOrderTraversalIterative(root);

    System.out.println("postOrderTraversalIterative: " +
    al.toString());
}
```

Output:

postOrderTraversalIterative: [2, 1, +, 3, *]

Complexity:

Time Complexity: O(n)   Space Complexity: O(1)

Explanation:

In the postOrderTraversalIterative() method, the root node is pushed into stack1 and then popped and pushed into stack2. The left and right node of the root node is pushed into stack1.

Iteratively, the last value from stack1 (right node) is popped and pushed into stack2. If there are any left or right node for this popped node, they are also pushed into stack1.

Once all nodes have been popped from stack1 and pushed to stack2, the values from stack2 are popped and added to output array al. The output array has the values in post order which is represented in reverse polish notation in this example.

s1 = [*]
postOrderTraversalIterative >>>>>

s1 = [], curr = *, s2=[*]

s1[+, 3]
s1 = [+], curr = 3, s2=[*, 3]
s1 = [], curr = +, s2=[*, 3, +]

s1[2, 1]

s1 = [2], curr = 1, s2=[*, 3, +, 1]
s1 = [], curr = 2, s2=[*, 3, +, 1, 2]

al=[2, 1, +, 3, *]

3.5.15

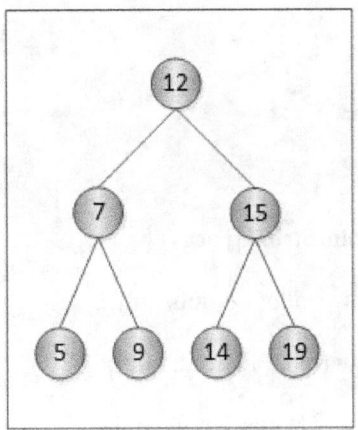

public class BinaryTreeDeepCopy {

```
    private static class Node {

            int value;
            Node left;
            Node right;

            Node(int val, Node l, Node r) {
                value = val;
                left = l;
                right = r;
            }

            Node deepCopy() {

            return new Node(value, left == null ? null : left.deepCopy(),
            right == null ? null : right.deepCopy());
            }
```

```
        }
}
```

What is the time complexity for the above deepCopy method?

a. O(1)
b. O(log n)
c. O(n)
d. O(n^2)

Ans: c

Answer Explanation:

Test Code:

```
public static void main(String [] args) {

        Node root = new Node(12, null, null);
        root.left = new Node(7, null, null);
        root.right = new Node(15, null, null);

        root.left.left = new Node(5, null, null);
        root.left.right = new Node(9, null, null);

        root.right.left = new Node(14, null, null);
        root.right.right = new Node(19, null, null);

        System.out.println("levelOrderTraversal root: ");
        levelOrderTraversal(root);

        Node root2 = root.deepCopy();
        System.out.println("\nAfter deepCopy, levelOrderTraversal
        root2: ");
        levelOrderTraversal(root2);
}
```

Output:

```
levelOrderTraversal root:
12
7 15
5 9 14 19
```

After deepCopy, levelOrderTraversal root2:
12
7 15
5 9 14 19

Complexity:

Time Complexity: O(n) Space Complexity: O(1)

Explanation:

In the deepCopy method, each time a new node is created, if the left and right nodes are not null, then the deepCopy method is called recursively to create a new node.

root.deepCopy() >>>>>
new Node(12) >>calls>> new Node(7) and new Node(15)

new Node(7) >>calls>> new Node(5) and new Node(9)

returns
new Node (5, null, null)
new Node (9, null, null)

returns
new Node (7, new Node(5, null,null), new Node(9, null,null))

new Node(15) >>calls>> new Node(14) and new Node(19)

returns
new Node (14, null, null)
new Node (19, null, null)

returns
new Node (15, new Node(14, null,null), new Node(19, null,null))

returns
new Node (12, new Node(7, ...), new Node(15, ...))

3.5.16

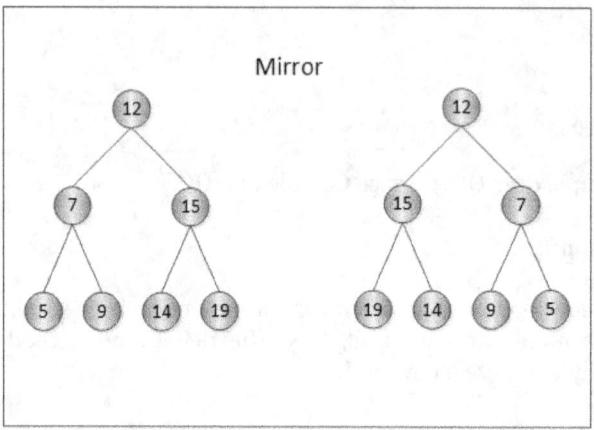

```
public class BinaryTreeEquals {

    private static class Node {

        int value;
        Node left;
        Node right;

        Node(int val) {
            value = val;
            left = null;
            right = null;
        }
    }

    public static boolean isEqual(Node n1, Node n2) {

        if(n1==null && n2==null) return true;

        if(n1==null || n2==null) return false;

        if(n1.value != n2.value) return false;

        else return (isEqual(n1.left, n2.left) &&
                    isEqual(n1.right, n2.right));
    }
```

```java
public static boolean isMirror(Node n1, Node n2) {

    if(n1==null && n2==null) return true;

    if(n1==null || n2==null) return false;

    if(n1.value != n2.value) return false;

    else return (isMirror(n1.right, n2.left) &&
                 isMirror(n1.left, n2.right));
}

public static void main(String [] args) {
    /*
     *
     *           12
     *      7           15
     *
     *   5    9     14   19
     *
     */
    Node root1 = new Node(12);
    root1.left = new Node(7);
    root1.right = new Node(15);

    root1.left.left = new Node(5);
    root1.left.right = new Node(9);

    root1.right.left = new Node(14);
    root1.right.right = new Node(19);

    /*
     *
     *           12
     *      15         7
     *
     *   19   14      9   5
     *
     */
    Node root2 = new Node(12);
    root2.left = new Node(15);
    root2.right = new Node(7);
```

```
        root2.left.left = new Node(19);
        root2.left.right = new Node(14);

        root2.right.left = new Node(9);
        root2.right.right = new Node(5);

        System.out.println("isEqual: " + isEqual(root1, root2));

        System.out.println("isMirror: " + isMirror(root1, root2));
    }
}
```

The above code on execution will return

a. true and false
b. false and true
c. true and true
d. false and false

Ans: b

Answer Explanation:

Output:

isEqual: false
isMirror: true

Complexity:

Time Complexity: O(n) Space Complexity: O(1)

Explanation:

In the main() method, binary tree root2 which is a mirror image of root1 is created and both these binary trees are passed as parameters to the isEqual and isMirror methods.

isEqual() returns false if root nodes are not equal. If root nodes are equal, then the left and right nodes are compared with the left and right nodes of the second binary tree.

isEqual() returns false as these two binary trees are not equal and isMirror() returns true as root2 is a mirror of root1.

isMirror(n1, n2) >>>>>

isMirror(12, 12) >>calls>> isMirror(15, 15) and isMirror(7, 7)

isMirror(15, 15) >>calls>> isMirror(19, 19) and isMirror(14, 14)
isMirror(7, 7) >>calls>> isMirror(9, 9) and isMirror(5, 5)

isMirror(19, 19), isMirror(14, 14), isMirror(9, 9) and isMirror(5, 5) >>calls>> isMirror(null, null)

isMirror(null, null) returns true

isMirror(19, 19), isMirror(14, 14), isMirror(9, 9) and isMirror(5, 5) return true

isMirror(15, 15) and isMirror(7, 7) return true
isMirror(12, 12) returns true

3.5.17

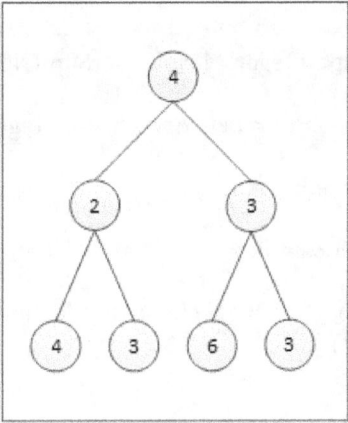

For the above binary tree, to implement a method that returns an arrayList with values [4, 5, 16] which is the sum of children in each level, the following traversal can be used.

a. level order traversal
b. in order traversal
c. pre order traversal
d. post order traversal

Ans: a

Answer Explanation:

Code:

```
public class BinaryTreeSumOfChildren {

    private static class Node {

        int value;
        Node left;
        Node right;

        Node(int val) {
            value = val;
            left = null;
            right = null;
        }
    }

    public static List<Integer> levelOrderSum(Node root) {

        List<Integer> al = new ArrayList<Integer>();

        if(root == null) return al;

        int levelNodes = 0;

        Queue<Node> q = new LinkedList<Node>();
        q.add(root);
        int sum = 0;

        while(!q.isEmpty()) {

            levelNodes = q.size();
```

```
            while(levelNodes > 0) {

                    Node n = (Node) q.remove();
                    sum += n.value;

                    if(n.left!=null) q.add(n.left);

                    if(n.right!=null) q.add(n.right);

                    levelNodes--;
            }
            al.add(sum);
            sum = 0;
        }
        return al;
    }
}
```

Test Code:

```
public static void main(String [] args) {
    /*
    *
    *           4
    *       2       3
    *
    *     4   3   6   3
    *
    */

    Node root = new Node(4);
    root.left = new Node(2);
    root.right = new Node(3);

    root.left.left = new Node(4);
    root.left.right = new Node(3);

    root.right.left = new Node(6);
    root.right.right = new Node(3);

    List<Integer> sumArray = levelOrderSum(root);
```

```
    System.outprintln("levelOrderSum: " +
    sumArray.toString());
}
```

Output:

levelOrderSum: [4, 5, 16]

Complexity:

Time Complexity: O(n) Space Complexity: O(1)

Explanation:

Traversal is searching through the tree in a particular order. Level order traversal is also called breath first search.

For level order traversal, the root node is first added to the queue. Then it's removed from the queue and the sum computed is added to the array. Next, the right and left nodes are added to the queue.

Sum of the right and left node values are added to the array after adding their children to the queue. All children in one level are summed iteratively and then added to the array.

```
/*
*
*            4
*      2        3
*
*    4   3    6   3
*
*/
root = 4
q = [ 4 ] >>>>>
levelNodes = 1, n = 4, q = [ 2, 3 ] , sum = 4, al = [4]

levelNodes = 2, n = 2, q = [ 3, 4, 3 ] , sum = 2, al = [4]
levelNodes = 1, n = 3, q = [ 4, 3, 6, 3 ] , sum = 5, al = [4, 5]

levelNodes = 4, n = 4, q = [ 3, 6, 3 ] , sum = 4, al = [4, 5]
levelNodes = 3, n = 3, q = [ 6, 3 ] , sum = 7, al = [4, 5]
```

levelNodes = 2, n = 6, q = [3] , sum = 13, al = [4, 5]
levelNodes = 1, n = 3, q = [ ], sum = 16, al = [4, 5, 16]
return [4, 5, 16]

3.5.18

What is the time complexity for converting a sorted array to a balanced binary search tree?

a. O(1)
b. O(log n)
c. O(n)
d. O(n^2)

Ans: c

Answer Explanation:

Code:

```
public class SortedArrayToBST {

    private static class Node {

        int value;
        Node left;
        Node right;

        Node(int val) {
            value = val;
            left = null;
            right = null;
        }
    }

    public static Node createBST(int [] arr) {

        if(arr.length < 1) return null;

        return createBST(arr, 0, arr.length-1);
    }
```

```java
public static Node createBST(int [] arr, int start, int end) {

    if(start > end) return null;

    int mid = (start + end)/2;

    Node root = new Node(arr[mid]);

    root.left = createBST(arr, start, mid-1);

    root.right = createBST(arr, mid+1, end);

    return root;
    }
}
```

Test Code:

```java
public static void main(String [] args) {

    int [] arr = {4, 5, 6, 7, 9, 12, 14};

    Node root = createBST(arr);

    System.out.println("levelOrderTraversal: ");
    levelOrderTraversal(root);
}
```

Output:

```
levelOrderTraversal:
7
5 12
4 6 9 14
```

Complexity:

Time Complexity: O(n) Space Complexity: O(1)

Explanation:

To convert a sorted array to a binary search tree, make the middle of the array as the root. Make the middle of the left half of the array as the left node and middle of the right half of the array as the right node recursively.

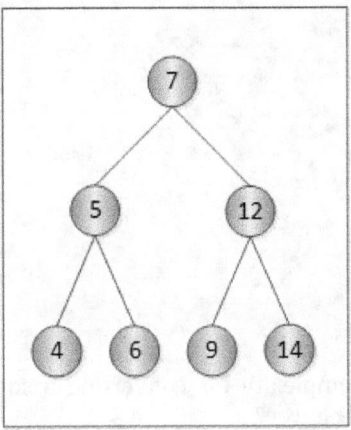

arr = [4, 5, 6, 7, 9, 12, 14] >>>>>
createBST(arr, 0, 6)
mid = 3, root = 7
7.left = createBST(arr, 0, 2)
7.right = createBST(arr, 4, 6)

createBST(arr, 0, 2) >> mid = 1, root = 5 >> returns 5
5.left = createBST(arr, 0, 0)
5.right = createBST(arr, 2, 2)

createBST(arr, 0, 0) >> mid = 0, root = 4 >> returns 4
createBST(arr, 2, 2) >> mid = 2, root = 6 >> returns 6

createBST(arr, 4, 6) >> mid = 5, root = 12 >> returns 12
12.left = createBST(arr, 4, 4)
12.right = createBST(arr, 6, 6)

createBST(arr, 4, 4) >> mid = 4, root = 9 >> returns 9
createBST(arr, 6, 6) >> mid = 6, root = 14 >> returns 14

3.5.19

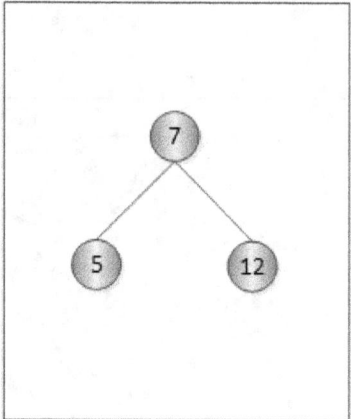

What is the time complexity for converting a sorted linked list to a balanced binary search tree?

a. O(1)
b. O(log n)
c. O(n)
d. O(n^2)

Ans: c

Answer Explanation:

Code:

```
public class SortedLinkedListToBST {

    private static class Node {

        int value;
        Node left;
        Node right;

        Node(int val) {
            value = val;
            left = null;
            right = null;
        }
}
```

```
    }

    public static Node createBST(LinkedList<Integer> head) {

        if((head==null) || (head.size() < 1)) return null;

        return createBST(head, 0, head.size()-1);
    }

    public static Node createBST(LinkedList<Integer> head, int start,
                                                          int end)
    {
        if(start > end) return null;

        int mid = (start + end)/2;

        Node left = createBST(head, start, mid-1);

        Node root = new Node(head.element());
        head.removeFirst();

        Node right = createBST(head, mid+1, end);

        root.left = left;
        root.right = right;

        return root;
    }
}
```

Test Code:

```
public static void main(String [] args) {

    LinkedList<Integer> head = new LinkedList<Integer>();

    head.add(0, 5);
    head.add(1, 7);
    head.add(2, 12);

    Node root = createBST(head);

    System.out.println("levelOrderTraversal: ");
```

levelOrderTraversal(root);
}

Output:

levelOrderTraversal:
7
5 12

Complexity:

Time Complexity: O(n) Space Complexity: O(1)

Explanation:

To convert a sorted linked list to a binary search tree, make the middle of the list as the root. Make the middle of the left half of the list as the left node and middle of the right half of the list as the right node recursively.

In the createBST method, first half of the LinkedList passed is used to create the left node. The middle element is used to create the root and the right half of the LinkedList is used to create the right node.

head = [5, 7, 12] >>>>>
createBST(head, 0, 2) >>
mid = 1
left = createBST(head, 0, 0)

createBST(head, 0, 0) >>
mid=0, left=null, root=5, head=7, right=null>> return 5

createBST(head, 0, 2) >>
mid = 1, left = 5, root = 7, head=12

right = createBST(head, 2, 2)
createBST(head, 2, 2) >>
mid=2, left=null, root=12, head=null, right=null>> return 12

createBST(head, 0, 2) >>
mid = 1, left = 5, root = 7, head=12, right = 12>> return 7

3.6 GRAPH AND TRIES

3.6.1

```java
public class GraphDemo {

    int vertexCount;

    LinkedList<Integer> [] adjList;

    GraphDemo(int vCount) {

        vertexCount = vCount;

        adjList = new LinkedList[vCount];

        for(int i=0; i<vCount; i++) {

            adjList[i]= new LinkedList<Integer>();
        }
    }

    public void addEdge(int vertex, int edge) {

        adjList[vertex].add(edge);
    }

    public void bfs(int vertex) {

        boolean [] visited = new boolean[vertexCount];

        LinkedList<Integer> queue = new LinkedList<Integer>();

        visited[vertex] = true;
        queue.add(vertex);

        while(!queue.isEmpty()) {

            int v = queue.poll();
            System.out.print(v + " ");
```

```
            Iterator<Integer> iter = adjList[v].iterator();

            while(iter.hasNext()) {

                v = iter.next();

                if(!visited[v]) {
                        visited[v]=true;
                        queue.add(v);
                }
            }
        }
    }

    public static void main(String [] args) {

        GraphDemo gd = new GraphDemo(5);
        gd.addEdge(0, 1);
        gd.addEdge(0, 2);
        gd.addEdge(1, 0);
        gd.addEdge(1, 3);
        gd.addEdge(2, 0);
        gd.addEdge(3, 2);
        gd.addEdge(3, 4);

        System.out.println("Breadth first search: ");
        gd.bfs(1);
    }
}
```

In the above code snippet of breadth first search for the graph, what will be printed in the output after 1 0 ?

a. 3
b. 2
c. 4
d. none of the above

Ans: a

Answer Explanation:

Output:

Breadth first search:
1 0 3 2 4

Complexity:

Time Complexity: O(V+E) Space Complexity: O(V+E)

Explanation:

The Graph in the above example is represented using an adjacency list. The adjacency list uses an array of linked list. Size of the array represents the number of vertices. So each vertex has a linked list and each list node represents the edge between this vertex and other vertices.

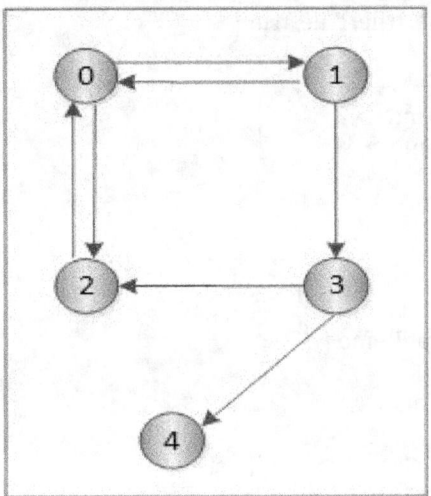

In the GraphDemo constructor, adjList which is an array of linked list is initialized using the vertex count passed. The addEdge method adds an edge to the vertex. The breadth first search bfs() method, uses the visited array to mark the visited vertices, as graphs may contain cycles. This prevents processing the same node again.

The vertex passed to the bfs() method is added to the queue. Iteratively the vertex is removed from the queue and printed followed by iterating through all the other vertices in the adjacency list which form the edges for this vertex. Each of the vertices are marked as visited is true and added to the queue.

In the above sample, when 1 is passed as the first vertex, the output printed is 10324.

```
bfs(1) >>>>>
visited[false, true, false, false, false]
queue = [ 1 ]
queue[ ] print>> 1
visited[true, true, false, true, false]

queue = [ 0, 3 ]
queue = [ 3 ] print>> 0
visited[true, true, true, true, false]

queue = [ 3, 2 ]
queue = [ 2 ] print>> 3
visited[true, true, true, true, true]

queue = [ 2, 4 ]
queue = [ 4 ] print>> 2
queue = [ ]   print>> 4
```

3.6.2

```java
public class GraphDemo {

    int vertexCount;

    LinkedList<Integer> [] adjList;

    GraphDemo(int vCount) {

        vertexCount = vCount;

        adjList = new LinkedList[vCount];

        for(int i=0; i<vCount; i++) {

            adjList[i]= new LinkedList<Integer>();
        }
    }
```

```java
public void addEdge(int vertex, int edge) {

    adjList[vertex].add(edge);
}
public void dfs(int vertex) {

    boolean [] visited = new boolean[vertexCount];

    dfs(vertex, visited);
}

public void dfs(int vertex, boolean [] visited) {

    visited[vertex] = true;
    System.out.print(vertex + " ");

    Iterator<Integer> iter = adjList[vertex].iterator();

    while(iter.hasNext()) {

        int v = iter.next();

        if(!visited[v]) {
            dfs(v, visited);
        }
    }
}

public static void main(String [] args) {

    GraphDemo gd = new GraphDemo(5);
    gd.addEdge(0, 1);
    gd.addEdge(0, 2);
    gd.addEdge(1, 0);
    gd.addEdge(1, 3);
    gd.addEdge(2, 0);
    gd.addEdge(3, 2);
    gd.addEdge(3, 4);

    System.out.println("Depth first search: ");
    gd.dfs(3);
}
}
```

In the above code snippet of depth first search for the graph, what will be printed in the output after 3 2 ?

a. 4
b. 1
c. 0
d. none of the above

Ans: c

Answer Explanation:

Output:

Depth first search:
3 2 0 1 4

Complexity:

Time Complexity: O(V+E) Space Complexity: O(V+E)

Explanation:

The Graph in the above program is represented using an adjacency list. The adjacency list uses an array of linked list. Size of the array represents the number of vertices. So each vertex has a linked list and each list node represents the edge between this vertex and other vertices.

In the GraphDemo constructor, adjList which is an array of linked list is initialized using the vertex count passed. The addEdge method adds an edge to the vertex. The depth first search dfs() method, uses the visited array to mark the visited vertices, as graphs may contain cycles. This prevents processing the same node again.

The first vertex is printed. All the vertices in the adjacency list that form the edges for this vertex are printed recursively after updating the visited array for this vertex. The DFS for this graph is 3 2 0 1 4 as the start vertex is 3.

dfs() >>>>>
dfs(3, visited) >>
visited[false, false, false, true, false], print>> 3

dfs(2, visited) >>
visited[false, false, true, true, false], print>> 2

dfs(0, visited) >>
visited[true, false, true, true, false], print>> 0

dfs(1, visited) >>
visited[true, true, true, true, false], print>> 1

dfs(4, visited) >>
visited[true, true, true, true, true], print>> 4

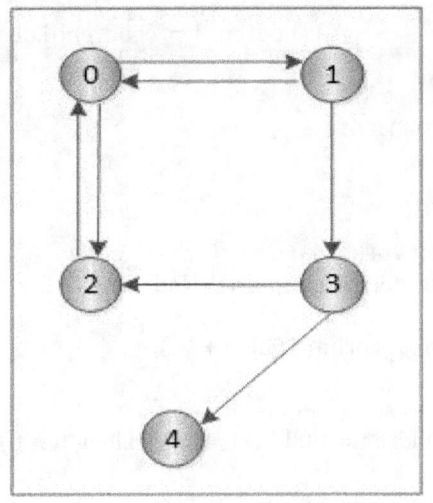

3.6.3

```
public class MultiwayTree {

    private static class Node {

        int value;
        Node [] children;

        Node(int val, Node [] c) {
```

```java
        value = val;
        children = c;
    }

    Node deepCopy() {

        Node n = new Node(value, null);

        if(children != null) {
            n.children = new Node[children.length];

            for(int i=0; i<children.length; i++) {

                n.children[i] =  children[i].deepCopy();
            }
        }
        return n;
    }
}

//print values of all children of children of a given node
public static void printChildren(Node n) {

    System.out.print(n.value + " ");

    //terminating condition
    if(n.children!= null && n.children.length > 0) {

        for(Node node : n.children) {
            printChildren(node);
        }
    }
}

public static void main(String [] args) {

    Node [] gc = new Node[2];

    gc[0] = new Node(100, null);
    gc[1] = new Node(200, null);

    Node [] c = new Node[2];
```

```
        c[0] = new Node(10, null);
        c[1] = new Node(20, gc);

        Node p = new Node(1, c);
        printChildren(p);

        Node n = p.deepCopy();

        System.out.println("\n\nAfter deepCopy: ");
        printChildren(n);
    }
}
```

In the above code snippet of deep copy for multiway tree, what will be the last line of the output?

a. 1 10 20 100 200
b. 1 10 20 100
c. 200 100 20 10 1
d. 100 20 10 1

Ans: a

Answer Explanation:

Output:

1 10 20 100 200

After deepCopy:
1 10 20 100 200

Complexity:

Time Complexity: O(n) Space Complexity: O(n)

Explanation:

The above multiway tree represents a tree with multiple nodes for its children. This structure is used in a Trie. Trie is a multiway tree where each node can contain up to 26 children.

In the above code, printChildren() method prints the value for a node and all children recursively. Similarly deepCopy() method makes a copy of the multiway tree recursively. In the main() method, parent p is created with children and grandchildren The values of all the nodes for this tree are printed followed by a deep copy.

3.6.4

```java
public class TrieDemo {

    private static class Node {

        Node [] children;

        boolean isEnd;

        Node() {
            children = new Node[26];
        }
    }

    public static void insert(String word, Node root) {

        Node curr = root;

        for(int i=0; i<word.length(); i++) {

            int index = word.charAt(i) - 'a';

            if(curr.children[index] == null) {

                curr.children[index] = new Node();

                curr = curr.children[index];
            }
            else
            {
                curr = curr.children[index];
            }
        }
        curr.isEnd = true;
    }
```

```java
public static boolean search(String word, Node root) {

    Node curr = searchNode(word, root);

    if(curr == null) return false;

    else if(curr.isEnd)  return true;

    return false;
}

public static Node searchNode(String word, Node root) {

    Node curr = root;

    for(int i=0; i<word.length(); i++) {

        int index = word.charAt(i) - 'a';

        if(curr.children[index] != null) {

            curr = curr.children[index];
        }
        else {
            return null;
        }
    }
    return curr;
}

public static void main(String [] args) {

    Node n = new Node();

    insert("ice", n);

    System.out.println("Search for ice: " + search("ice", n));

    System.out.println("Search for jet: " + search("jet", n));
}
}
```

In the above code snippet of insert and search in the Trie, what will be the last line of the output?

a. true
b. false
c. true or false
d. none of the above

Ans: b

Answer Explanation:

Output:

Search for ice: true
Search for jet: false

Complexity:

Time Complexity: O(L) Space Complexity: O(L)

Explanation:

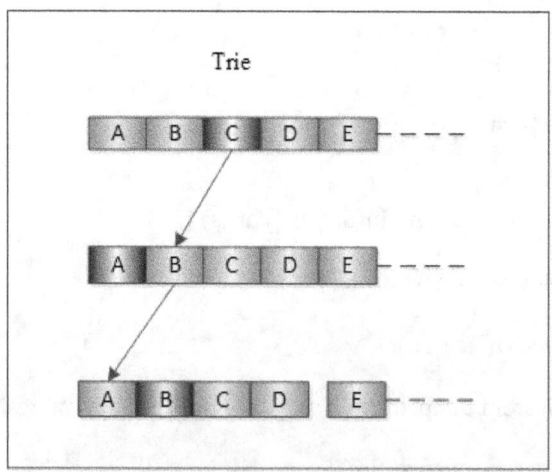

Tries are data structures based on prefix of a string. They are used for Re'trie'val of data. It's a multiway tree where each node can contain up to 26 children for 26 letters of the English alphabet.

Complexity for insert and search string in a Trie is O(L), where L is the length of the word. Search and insert operation in Tries are very fast but it requires a lot of memory as each node has many children.

In the insert() method, iteratively each character in the word is used to compute the index, by subtracting the ASCII value of the character from the ASCII value of character 'a'. So 'a' will be represented by index zero and z by index 25.

A new node is created for the child in the corresponding index for the alphabet. Next, the children of this node is accessed to create a new node for the next alphabet in the word iteratively.

Once the node for the last character has been created, the isEnd variable is set to true. If the nodes were already created for the characters, they are simply iterated till the isEnd variable is set.

Similarly in the search() method, for each node, the child with the index corresponding to the character is checked if the valid node is present for all the characters in the word. If the valid node is not present, then false is returned. If isEnd is true for the last character, then true is returned.

In the above code, word 'ice' is inserted into the Trie and search for this word returns true, while search for 'jet' returns false.